The Witches' Runes

About Josephine Winter

Josephine Winter has been a witch of some flavour for most of her life, beginning in Norse-inspired Heathenry and later the Alexandrian tradition of Wicca. She holds degrees in education, literature, and the arts. Over the last few decades, she has been a regular volunteer and organiser at various Pagan and witchy events around Australia. More recently, she became a cofounder of Lepus Lumen, a teaching collective of covens, outercourts, and solo practitioners. She lives in country Victoria, in Australia's leafy southeast.

About Jason Tremain

Jason Tremain is an Australian musician, teacher, and writer whose work explores the meeting points of music, ritual, and animism. An initiate of Alexandrian Witchcraft, he has taught and presented on witchcraft, occult traditions, and musicology, bringing together research and lived practice. His writing reflects a deep interest in creativity, tradition, and the ways people find meaning in the natural world. Visit him at Arawnbel.wordpress.com.

To Write to the Authors

If you wish to contact the author or would like more information about this book, please write to the authors in care of Llewellyn Worldwide Ltd. and we will forward your request. Both the authors and the publisher appreciate hearing from you and learning of your enjoyment of this book and how it has helped you. Llewellyn Worldwide Ltd. cannot guarantee that every letter written to the author can be answered, but all will be forwarded. Please write to:

Josephine Winter
Jason Tremain
℅ Llewellyn Worldwide
2143 Wooddale Drive
Woodbury, MN 55125-2989

Please enclose a self-addressed stamped envelope for reply, or $1.00 to cover costs. If outside the U.S.A., enclose an international postal reply coupon.

Many of Llewellyn's authors have websites with additional information and resources. For more information, please visit our website at https://www.llewellyn.com.

Praise for *The Witches' Runes*

"A wonderful book which opens the door to a mysterious, almost forgotten system that has lasted through the ages and deserves to be better known."

—**DOLORES ASHCROFT-NOWICKI**, author of *The Ritual Magic Workbook, Magical Use of Thought Forms,* and others

"*The Witches' Runes* teaches a versatile and deceptively simple divination system. Readers will find practical, down-to-earth answers to their questions in these pages, as Tremain and Winter present a modern take on a form of divination uniquely suited to a witch's needs."

—**JACK CHANEK**, author of *Tarot for the Magically Inclined*

"An accessible, practical, working guide for learning a unique system of divination. Tremain and Winter lay out history, folklore, myth, and magic to help the would-be Witches' Runes diviner become intimate with these special stones. This unique and elegant system is given a home in these pages and many will find sustenance and inspiration here. A magical guide to mysterious symbols that will offer clarity, power, and meaning."

—**FIO GEDE PARMA**, author of *Ecstatic Witchcraft* and *The Witch Belongs to the World*

"*The Witches' Runes* by Jason Tremain and Josephine Winter is nothing short of a triumph! This is an authentic and inspiring work dedicated to a rare and powerful divination system rooted in the lore and praxis of magic and Witchcraft. Within these pages, the authors uncover a seldom-seen method of magical meaning-making! Not only rare but one that honors and expands upon the work of luminaries such as Dolores Ashcroft-Nowicki, Gardnerian High Priestess Patricia Crowther, and Australian Craft pioneer Simon Goodman. I found this book to be much more than a manual. This book is a living, breathing invitation into the ongoing practice of uncovering the mystery of the Witches' Runes. Tremain and Winter guide the reader through every facet of the stones from creation to maintenance and symbolism.... Their words don't just inform; they activate the unseen, carrying forward sacred threads of witch-lore into their own practice. An indispensable, spirited, and wholly magical resource!

—**NATHAN KING**, author of *Awakening the Witchblood*

The Witches' Runes

History, Creation, and Use

Josephine Winter
Jason Tremain

Woodbury, Minnesota

First Edition
First Printing, 2026

Book design by Christine Ha
Cover design by Shannon McKuhen
Interior illustrations by the Llewellyn Art Department

Library of Congress Cataloging-in-Publication Data (Pending)
ISBN: 978-0-7387-8177-8

Llewellyn Publications
A Division of Llewellyn Worldwide Ltd.
2143 Wooddale Drive
Woodbury, MN 55125-2989
www.llewellyn.com

Printed in the United States of America

GPSR Representation:
UPI-2M PLUS d.o.o., Medulićeva 20, 10000 Zagreb, Croatia,
matt.parsons@upi2mbooks.hr

Other Books by Josephine Winter

Fire Magic

Witchcraft Discovered

Old knowledge, if it be true knowledge, is never lost.
—Dolores Ashcroft-Nowicki

Contents

Foreword

Romani Runes

by Dolores Ashcroft-Nowicki

I was born and grew up in the Channel Islands, which lie between the coasts of Britain and France. During World War II, when the Germans invaded the Islands, I was evacuated with my parents. We settled in the Wirral, a place where the veil between the worlds is very thin. Halfway between the village and the local school, which I attended, was an open moor, and here, twice a year, a family of Romani used to make a wayside camp.

There is a tradition in my family that, on my father's side, we have a strain of Romani blood, and we never turned away any of the traveling folk from our doors. It was, therefore, only a matter of time before I was a frequent caller at the camp fire. There I met Vashti, an ancient grandmother with whom I struck up a friendship. I learnt a little of the Romani language and could make an attempt to *rakker romani* (speak Romani) with the families. But to me, the most important lessons were those in palmistry and the art of *dukkerin*, or fortune-telling. I could listen to Vashti for as long as she would talk and never tire.

Once she told me that, as I was one of the sea folk (i.e., an islander), I should know about the "Stones O'Leary." Many years later, when I was more knowledgeable in ancient lore, I realized that this name was what common usage had made of the Stones of Llyr, the ancient Celtic sea god.

Vashti told me that long ago, Llyr, or Leary, had given ten stones of the sea to a woman who had hidden him from a hunter while he was in the shape of a seal. He taught her how to gather them and mark them and told her that they would tell her the future.

The old woman told me that one of the ten had been lost and that, since then, although the stones would still speak, they would never tell the whole of the picture. She also told me of other kinds of "Telling Stones." Some were Earth Stones, some were made of slips of wood, and still others were of jewels, though these were a special kind. Each jewel had to be different and had to be received as a gift, each one from a different person—male if the recipient was a woman, female if it was a man.

It was from her grandmother that Vashti had learnt of the stones, the different kinds and the making and using of them. Someone who loved the lore of earth used Kerry Stones (stones of Ceridwen, the earth goddess). These must be searched for at a time of day that is neither light nor dark and should be taken from just below the surface of the earth. Only an earth person could use Earth Stones, just as only a sea person could use the Sea Stones. All this old knowledge was given to me freely from the store of folk memory of the old Romani woman.

It took many visits to wheedle all the details from Vashti, but I soaked it all up like a sponge. All through the weeks of their stay I learnt about the "Talking Stones" and a lot more besides.

After they left that year, I never saw Vashti again. She died down south and was burnt along with her old Vardo in clothes that had been turned inside out, as was the custom in her family.

The stones faded from memory until one summer day, walking by the sea and throwing stones into the wave, I picked up one with a pattern on it. This awakened a memory, and the old symbols flooded back. I looked down and found another but with a different pattern on it—and there, with the element of Llyr washing around my feet, the tenth symbol fell into place. There had to be an Eye Stone, a stone that symbolized the "I" of the querent—which gave the others something to react to. I started looking around me, all the old instructions coming back. It was as if Vashti was beside me again.

I took my sea booty home and painted them. Placing the Eye Stone some way away, I cupped the others in my hands and whispered the old rhyme:

Stones O'Leary,
Stones O'Leary,
tell me truly,
tell me clearly,
give to me an answer true,
show me what I am to do.

Let my Eye see clear and bright
that I may keep my future right.

I tried many questions that night, and every time, the stones answered truly until at last I threw them and each one lay turned over. I took the hint and placed them in their leather bag and put them away for the night.

Old knowledge, if it be true knowledge, is never lost. This I have proved to my own satisfaction. Anyone can make and use the Rune Stones. The most difficult part is just finding out if one is better working with Earth or Sea. I have found that nearly everyone falls into one or the other of the two. The symbols are simple and no skill with painting is required. In fact, the cruder the better for reasons that I think are because they are more like those of early times and so draw on that part of the race memory.

This lovely book by Josephine Winter and Jason Tremain digs deeper into the mystery of the Stones. It's an excellent guide to learning, and using, the Romani Runes—these days widely known as Witches' Runes. The Stones will grow closer to you, and a link will be formed that will serve you well. Try it and I wish you *Kushto Bok* (Good Luck) with them.

Introduction

As we sit, the world falls away and the weight of the stones settles into our hands. The familiar shapes and markings of the Witches' Runes shift gently as we prepare to cast them, a quiet thrill blooming in the back of our minds. Each rune is alive with possibility. There is a ritual to this moment, an art—a familiar sequence of grounding, focusing, and releasing, from settling on the right question to that pulse of intent travelling from fingers to the stones themselves. Rolling the stones in our hands, we close our eyes and hold our question. Slowly, we say the quaint jingle that accompanies this method of reading before breathing our intention into the stones as one final act of communication. When finally ready, we cast the runes. They scatter across the cloth, coming to rest in a pattern born of chance and yet layered with purpose and meaning. Something shifts in that moment. The symbols speak, their messages woven between past and future, intuition and memory.

This book is an invitation into the world of the Witches' Runes: a journey that is both within and without, a dance between intuition and action. Here you will encounter the runes both as a collective system and as individual symbols, each with its own distinct energy and tale to tell. Together we will explore their meanings and symbols, their mythic roots, and the ways they move us to act and reflect. You'll be guided through meditations that deepen your relationship with each rune, allowing its essence to speak directly to you. You'll come to understand the language of the runes and develop a profound connection to them, one that deepens with each reading.

How We Met the Runes

Many witches who come to the practice these days start their foray into divinatory runes with a set of stones depicting the Elder Futhark, a runic alphabet and writing system adopted by modern Norse Pagans as a form of divination. Our own paths were not too different. Jason was introduced to reading the tarot by his uncle at an early age, fuelling an already pronounced fascination with the occult. It was as a teenager that he encountered Paul Huson's *Mastering Witchcraft*, which introduced him to geomancy and eventually led him to seek out a coven. Josie's first tarot lessons were as a tween in a shopping mall crystal shop, and she fell in love with reading the Elder Futhark in the first Pagan group she joined as a young adult.

It wasn't until we started training in coven-based craft that we were introduced to the Witches' Runes, also known as the Stones O'Leary. Neither of us had come across this system, consisting of just ten marked stones, and we both had backgrounds in reading in many other formats, all much more complex. It was quite the refreshing gear shift and challenge to learn to read with only these ten images, and to do so in an accurate and helpful way.

An Act of Creation

The journey to create a set of Witches' Runes—and learning how to read them—is more than an intellectual pursuit, and it will take you beyond passive understanding of the divinatory method. This pursuit is a call to creation, and you will learn to bring the runes to life, crafting your own set stone by stone, each one imbued with your intent and energy. These will not be mere tools of divination; they will become allies and guides, mirrors and mysteries, as you learn to read them and, in turn, read yourself through them.

This act of creation is not simply a practical process either. It is a ritual in and of itself. The process of creating each rune will ask something of you—intention, focus, and a willingness to connect deeply with the forces these symbols represent. As you carve or paint each one, you'll find your own insights growing and your awareness deepening. In forging the runes, you begin to forge yourself.

The act of making your own rune set offers unique benefits. Each rune becomes a vessel for personal insight, a channel for wisdom drawn from both inner intuition and the deep well of human myth. Working closely with the symbols, you will find they begin to reveal aspects of yourself you may not have encountered before. This journey offers you a lens into self-discovery, a mirror held up by the runes to reveal strengths, patterns, and possibilities you carry within. Through their symbols, you'll find support, challenge, and guidance that grows in clarity with every reading.

How to Use This Book

We designed this book to guide you step-by-step through the process of creating, learning, connecting with, and working with a unique divinatory system. Whether you're a beginner or an experienced practitioner, you'll find practical exercises and insights to help deepen your understanding and relationship with the runes. It's a good idea to have a journal handy as you work through this book, as there will be specific prompts for each stone.

The book is divided into two main parts: an introduction to the rune system and an exploration of each rune.

In the first section, you'll learn the history, structure, and overall philosophy behind the Witches' Runes. This section lays the foundation for your work, introducing you to the runes' origins and their symbolism, as well as how they fit into broader magical and divinatory practices.

In the second section, each rune will be presented individually, offering a detailed exploration of its meaning, symbolism, and practical uses. This is the heart of the book, where you will deepen your connection to the runes one by one. Each chapter is dedicated to a single rune, providing exercises, meditations, and prompts to help you engage fully with its energy.

In the final chapter of the book, we'll look at some of the different ways that readings can be performed with this system. It might be tempting to skip ahead to this section, but do try to persist with the exploration chapters first: The effectiveness of this system is reliant on your relationship with your own set of stones.

How to Work Through the Book

You are invited to progress through this book at your own pace, one rune at a time. Here's how you can approach it.

As you explore each rune, you'll be encouraged to physically create or choose a stone for it. This could involve carving, painting, or marking a stone with the rune's symbol. The act of creating the rune stone will help you bond with the rune's energy on a deeper level.

Each rune section will include exercises designed to help you connect with its meaning. These may involve guided meditations, journaling prompts, or small ritual practices. Working through these exercises will allow you to develop a personal relationship with each rune.

By the time you've worked through each rune chapter, you'll have not only crafted a complete set of Witches' Runes but also established a personal, energetic connection to each stone. This gradual approach ensures that your understanding of the runes is built from hands-on experience, rather than just theoretical knowledge.

Suggested Pace

Take your time with each rune. Some readers may feel drawn to focus on one rune for a week or more, while others may choose to explore at a quicker pace. There is no rush—your goal is to fully immerse yourself in the energy and symbolism of each rune before moving on to the next.

Working with the Full Set

Once you've completed the journey through all the runes, the book will provide guidance on how to use the full rune set in divination, spellwork, and other magical practices. By this stage, you'll have developed a strong, intuitive sense of how each rune communicates, both on its own and in relation to others.

This book is both a guide and a tool to support your personal exploration of the Witches' Runes. As you move through each chapter, you will be creating your own unique rune set while developing a deeper understanding of this ancient system. May your journey be one of discovery, insight, and empowerment.

Getting Started

Whether you are a seasoned practitioner or new to witchcraft, by the end of this book you will own a divination set that is truly yours—crafted your own hands and your own spirit, resonant with your energy. This set of runes is not just an assemblage of stones or symbols but a deeply personal set of tools, one that will continue to evolve and deepen with use. As you draw from your set of Witches' Runes, you will hold a map for insight, creativity, and transformation—a powerful companion on your path, bringing the profound mysteries of these ancient symbols into the heart of your own life. Welcome to your journey with the Witches' Runes.

Before we begin, it is important that we mention a historical detail about these stones. They were at one time called *Gypsy Runes*. The term first appeared in an article written by Dolores Ashcroft-Nowicki in the quarterly magazine *Quadriga* and was used intermittently in subsequent publications discussing this divination set, as well as its various iterations. This is not a term considered appropriate today and not one we will be using outside of the stones' historical context. We now use the more widely accepted term *Gypsy, Roma, and Traveller* (*GRT*) for what would have been one of several diverse ethnic groups that have a shared history of nomadism in Europe and have been written about previously as Gypsies.

Chapter One
Discovering the Witches' Runes

The Witches' Runes first appeared in the writings of psychic and occultist Dolores Ashcroft-Nowicki, who wrote about a system of fortune-telling using gypsy runes, also known as the Stones O'Leary, in 1977. The stones have since been mentioned in the published work and private materials of many authors and witches.

The stones' imagery—an eye, the sun, the moon, three rings, birds in flight, water, grain, two crossed spears, a star, and a sickle—is simple enough that readings are fairly easy to perform. Despite this simplicity, and in part as a result of it, the Witches' Runes provide the reader with complex and rich layers of meaning that are further elaborated by the relationships between the stones. The depth of your relationship with the stones will directly impact the stories they tell, and the work in this book will greatly assist in building the desired connection.

Dolores Ashcroft-Nowicki

Dolores Ashcroft-Nowicki, born 1929, is a prominent British occultist, author, and teacher known for her extensive work in the Western Mystery Tradition. She was born into a family with strong esoteric connections, being described as a third-generation psychic.

Ashcroft-Nowicki began her formal training in the occult with W. E. Butler, a well-known occultist and founder of the Servants of the Light (SOL), an esoteric school devoted to the Western Mysteries. She continued to develop her knowledge through a variety of Western magical traditions, including ceremonial magic, Kabbalah, and ritual practice. In 1976, following Butler's retirement, she became the director of the SOL, a position she held until 2018. Her approach combines practical occultism with a deep understanding of symbolic systems and ancient traditions.[1]

A prolific author, her books include *The Shining Paths, The Ritual Magic Workbook,* and *The Servants of the Light,* among others. Her works often focus on accessible methods of magical training, visualisation, and ritual structure. Ashcroft-Nowicki has been a respected voice in the Western esoteric community for decades and is widely regarded as a key figure in the continuation of the Golden Dawn lineage, as well as in the teaching of magic, mysticism, and spiritual development.[2]

In the course of her publishing career, Ashcroft-Nowicki introduced a divination system that she called Gypsy Runes. In 1977, she published an essay on the system in *Quadriga,* a quarterly magazine run by British occultist and ritual magician Gareth Knight. The essay was later published in the *Golden Dawn Journal* and also in a "highlight reel" collection of essays from the journal edited by Tabatha and Chic Cicero.

In the article, Ashcroft-Nowicki recounted the time she spent away from her home in the Channel Islands during World War II. During that period, she and her family lived in the Wirral, a peninsula in North West England whose boundaries include Dee Estuary to the west, the Mersey Estuary to the east, and Liverpool Bay to the north. Ashcroft-Nowicki described the Wirral as a strange place. "At that time it was all open country," she wrote, "and the walk [home from school] was an eerie one, especially on misty Autumn days when the days drew in."[3]

It was during this time that Ashcroft-Nowicki says she met the family of GRT people who made a wayside camp nearby twice a year as they passed through the area. Even at a young age, she was enchanted by these people, possibly because of her father's stories about his family having "a strain of Gypsy blood," and sought to meet and interact with them.[4]

Her first encounters with the GRT family were not all smooth: Ashcroft-Nowicki writes about having been chided for coming between a man and his fire

---

1. "History."
2. Llewellyn, "Dolores Ashcroft-Nowicki," accessed February 2025, https://www.llewellyn.com/author.php?author_id=2054.
3. Ashcroft-Nowicki, "The Gypsy Runes," 231.
4. Ashcroft-Nowicki, "The Gypsy Runes," 231.

and for approaching a fire for the first time without permission. Her first positive interactions were with an old woman named Vashti, who in subsequent visits to the area taught Ashcroft-Nowicki about a fortune-telling method using stones. Vashti had learned the system from her grandmother and called them sea stones or the Stones O'Leary.[5]

Kerry Stones, Stones O'Leary, Stones of Llŷr

Vashti told Ashcroft-Nowicki the story of a shape-shifting character she called Leary. Long ago, he had gifted ten stones to a woman who had hidden him from a hunter while he was in his more vulnerable seal shape. Leary taught the woman how to collect and mark the stones in order to make additional sets. He taught her the magic words to make the stones "speak."

Vashti also said that the markings and meaning of one of the ten stones had been lost. "Since then," she said, "although the stones would still speak, they would never tell the whole of the picture."[6]

It wasn't until years later that Ashcroft-Nowicki made the connection between Leary and the Welsh mythological figure Llŷr. Many scholars assert that this name is taken from the Irish sea god, father of Manannán mac Lir, who himself is king of the Otherworld and one of the Tuatha Dé Danann.[7]

The wisdom that Vashti shared with Ashcroft-Nowicki included lore about sea people and earth people, and how each type of person should find, make, and use the stones. Sea people used the Stones O'Leary, while only people of the earth could use Kerry stones, named for the goddess Cerridwen. Vashti called Ashcroft-Nowicki a "sea" person because of her close affinity with the Channel Islands.

Ashcroft-Nowicki and Vashti eventually went their separate ways and Vashti later passed away. As she grew up and went off to work, Ashcroft-Nowicki all but forgot about the stones. It wasn't until a friend and fellow occultist showed her some stones purchased from an old sea captain that the stones were raised in her memory.

However, it would be years again before, when walking on a beach, she would have a revelation about the tenth "lost" stone: It was the Eye stone, the stone that

5. Ashcroft-Nowicki, "The Gypsy Runes," 231.
6. Ashcroft-Nowicki, "The Gypsy Runes," 232.
7. Mackillop, *A Dictionary of Celtic Mythology*, 301.

often represents the subject of a reading. "With the Element of Llyr washing around my feet," she wrote, "the tenth symbol fell into place. There had to be an EYE Stone, a Stone that symbolized the 'I' of the Querent—which gave the others something to react to."[8]

With the set completed and the rhyme revealed, Ashcroft-Nowicki now had a workable system of divination, one that she would teach to some of her students and that they would pass on, and on and on until this fascinating set of stones was being used all over the world.

Interest Expands

The stones came to Australia through several different teachers. Some of them had been trained by Simon Goodman, an Australian occultist credited with setting up the first lineaged British Traditional Wiccan covens in Australia in the late 1970s. The stones formed a part of an open training program that he ran in several different places around the country.

Goodman was a prominent figure in the Alexandrian Wiccan tradition, playing a significant role in promoting the craft in Australia. He was responsible for establishing covens across multiple states and contributed to the formation of various Wiccan groups. Goodman founded the Covenantus Quercus in the 1970s, a group that has since expanded across Australia. He also helped set up several annual Pagan festivals in the eastern states that continue to this day.

Goodman maintained strong connections with Alexandrian and Gardnerian groups both in the United Kingdom and throughout Europe, contributing to the development and recognition of these traditions abroad. He was a passionate advocate for clarifying the distinctions between Wicca and other occult practices, such as Satanism, especially in the public eye through media engagements. His dedication to the craft is evident not only in his role as a high priest but also in his significant work within the wider Pagan community. His legacy continues to influence many covens in Australia and beyond.

While documentary evidence suggests that Goodman began teaching the Witches' Runes in Australia in the late 1970s, it is not entirely clear where he picked them up. It is possible that the stones came through a connection with British witch and author Patricia Crowther, who also wrote about the stones, though

8. Ashcroft-Nowicki, "The Gypsy Runes," 234.

her system differed in several key ways. These differences included the use of eight stones instead of ten and the absence of some symbols, such as the sickle, which were substituted by signs unique to the iteration. These differences are explored in more detail further in the chapter. However the stones came to be introduced to Australian occultists, the system became a part of craft lore in the country and has since accumulated its own stories and varied practices. In other parts of the world, the stones have also been widely shared between different practitioners, and there are now countless variations of this fascinating system out there.

In North America, a version of the Ashcroft-Nowicki runes was combined with some runes from another set first written about by Dana Corby and introduced to a broader audience by the author Susan Sheppard. Some later texts credit Sheppard as creating this system, and most sets called Witches' Runes available to buy online are the Sheppard version of the runes.

The stones' history is complex, fragmentary, and woven through several tellings, with at least two versions of the origin story. Some of the lore explored throughout this book, particularly around the process of creating the stones, emerged from the many unnamed people who used the system after it was introduced in Australia. Other lore shows clear links to the origin stories provided by Ashcroft-Nowicki or subsequent proponents of their use. The connection to a god of the sea can be seen reflected in the use of river stones or pebbles collected at the seashore and serves as an example of how traditions surrounding the stones have evolved or transformed over time.

The Witches' Runes are intended to be intuitive and personal, encouraging the practitioner to rely on their own inner wisdom and connection to the symbols during readings. They also reflect Ashcroft-Nowicki's eclectic approach to the occult, as she blended traditional esoteric systems with her own innovations to create a practical and accessible tool for spiritual exploration and divination. They are an example of her broader work in the Western Mystery Tradition, where she has continually sought to make occult wisdom applicable to modern spiritual seekers.

Tracking the Evolution of Two Modern Systems

The set of Witches' Runes we write about in this book is one of several similar sets and systems that appeared in the second half of the twentieth century and beyond. When we look at these in the order they were written about, a distinct pattern emerges. Following is a sampling of some notable mentions of the Witches' Runes throughout the twentieth and twenty-first centuries. This is not an exhaustive list, but it gives us a good idea of how these systems have evolved and continue to do so.

1975: Dana Corby

In 1975, two years before Ashcroft-Nowicki's article was first published, Dana Corby, North American priestess of the Mohsian tradition of Wicca and one of the founders of the Covenant of the Goddess, also published an article in the United States Neopagan journal *Crystal Well* about a set of similar rune stones.[9] Corby's rune set had fourteen runes, while Ashcroft-Nowicki's had ten.

The images on Corby's runes are man, woman, love, family, home, gifts, money, possessions, poison, disordered thoughts, war, death, comfort, and fire. The list differs greatly from Ashcroft-Nowicki's images: eye, moon, star, crossed spears, waves, grain, birds, sickle, rings, and sun.

For the most part, Corby's images are created with straight, simple lines in a fashion reminiscent of the Elder Futhark. In fact, six of the runes are exactly the same as Elder Futhark runes and carry similar meanings: Eiwaz (Death), Elhaz (Man), Gebo (Gifts), Kenaz (Fire), Othala (Possessions), and Wunjo (Comfort).

Corby later expanded her article into a book titled *The Witches' Runes: A Traditional Divination System*. The same system also appears uncredited in Ed Fitch's *Magical Rites from the Crystal Well*, which is a collection of rituals and writing from the *Crystal Well* magazine, with slight variations in the War and Disordered Thoughts runes.[10]

In her book, Corby says that the system was passed to her in 1972 as part of her original training in the craft. Corby had researched the history of the system, and while she supposes their origin to be British "oral lore," she couldn't trace it back any further than her own teacher, Lady Sara.[11]

Given the timeline of her publication, this accounting would make sense. The runes were most likely being transmitted orally until Corby published a version of them in America.

9. "About Dana Corby," *Patheos* (blog).
10. Fitch, *Magical Rites from The Crystal Well*, 9.
11. Corby, *The Witches' Runes*, 15.

Similar to the Ashcroft-Nowicki set, the set of runes given to Corby by Lady Sara were large black-and-white Mexican beach pebbles with the runes painted onto them. When making her own sets, Corby switched to tumbled glass, which was more easily available, before switching back to stones collected from the beach when she moved somewhere more coastal.[12]

1981: Patricia Crowther

In the early 1980s, several years after Ashcroft-Nowicki's article was published, United Kingdom author and high priestess in the Gardnerian tradition Patricia Crowther outlined a system she called rune stones, comprised of eight stones. Crowther explained that there were this many because eight was "the number of the craft."[13] Several of Crowther's stones are similar or identical to those in the system written about by Ashcroft-Nowicki; there is a Sun stone, a Moon stone, a rune marked with interlocking rings called the Love stone, a rune with crossed spears, one with curling waves that Crowther calls the Relatives stone, and a Birds stone. Instead of a Wheat/Harvest stone, this set has a Lucky stone, depicting a sprouting stalk or an ear of corn.[14]

Ashcroft-Nowicki's Star, Sickle, and Eye stones do not appear in this set. Instead, there is a single black stone cut or painted with a symbol similar to a capital *H*. This stone carries divinatory meanings similar to those of the Sickle stone in the Ashcroft-Nowicki set: grief, partings, and misfortune.

While Crowther does not state her source or provide a history for the runes, the advice she gives suggests Ashcroft-Nowicki as a common source. Goodman was already teaching this divination system in Australia at the time *Lid Off the Cauldron* was being written, which suggests that both he and Crowther learned of the stones from Ashcroft-Nowicki around the same time. Further, much of the lore associated with Crowther's runes is very close to what has been received with the Ashcroft-Nowicki version of the stones in Australia. For example, Crowther said that "suitable stones for this type of divination can be collected from the beach, or even an old quarry, though, personally, I think you have a much wider

12. Corby, *The Witches' Runes*, 39.
13. Crowther, *Lid Off the Cauldron*, 110.
14. Crowther, *Lid Off the Cauldron*, 112.

choice on the sea-shore."[15] This is similar to what Ashcroft-Nowicki wrote about her Stones O'Leary—sea stones—in 1977.

Some of the key lore from Crowther's writings includes the idea of not bothering the runes repeatedly for answers to the same questions. Much of the writing implies a certain character to the divination set, which grows impatient with trivial or inconsequential questioning. People may find, as Crowther noted, that the stones stop communicating with you in the event that you pester them too much. Another piece of lore about the relationship between the reader and their runes states that you should avoid having other people handle or read the stones as much as possible. To neglect this could lead to the runes no longer communicating honestly with their owner.

1989: Scott Cunningham

American witch and author Scott Cunningham mentions a set of runes similar to Corby's in several of his works, most notably his bestseller *Wicca: A Guide for the Solitary Practitioner*, which was first published in 1989. In this book, Cunningham writes about a set of twelve rune stones: Home, Possessions, Love, Poison, Wealth, Disordered Thoughts, Woman, Man, Gift, Comfort, Death, and War. The symbols can be painted onto flat-sided stones and cast to tell the future.[16]

Many of the symbols are the same or quite similar to those on Corby's runes, albeit with an extra line or square added here or there, though the Family and Fire runes are omitted. The divinatory meanings are almost identical too. A few stones look quite different: Cunningham's Love rune more closely resembles Corby's Poison. Death looks more like the Gifts rune from Corby's set. Cunningham's Wealth bears no resemblance to Corby's Money, though the two carry the same divinatory meaning, likewise with the War rune in both sets.

There is no citation or mention of sources or origins of the runes in Cunningham's writings. Despite the absence of a clear textual reference, there are obvious connections to the earlier publications by Ashcroft-Nowicki and Crowther. These continuities include the advice to collect stones from a riverbed or the seashore and to paint the symbols onto one side, as well as reading by tossing the stones and noting only those stones that land face up. In interpreting the reading,

---

15. Crowther, *Lid Off the Cauldron*, 110.
16. Cunningham, *Wicca*, 194–96.

Cunningham also mentions combinations of runes based on their proximity in a spread. It appears, from what he writes about this divination set and the symbols he used, that Cunningham blended aspects of Ashcroft-Nowicki's Gypsy Runes with elements from the Futhark rune sets to create his own system. Considering the similarities between this set and the system described by Corby in 1975, it would appear Cunningham was familiar with either her work or the reproduction by Ed Fitch, which was published five years before *Wicca*.

1989: Rhiannon Ryall

Rhiannon Ryall is the pseudonym of English-born Australian author Maureen Mileham, who in the mid-1990s achieved notoriety for her controversial claims regarding the existence of a group of Wiccans living in England's West Country during the 1940s. These claims first came to the attention of Wiccans and academics with Capall Bann's publication of her book *West Country Wicca: A Journal of the Old Religion* in the United Kingdom in 1993.

In this book, which had been published in the United States some years earlier in 1989, Ryall describes a set of ten divinatory "tell stones" moulded from clay. Just like the Ashcroft-Nowicki stones, Ryall's "tell stones" were read with one stone representing the querent, and in order of importance going out from the querent stone. Face down stones were discarded, and groups of stones were read in conjunction with one another, as they are in the Ashcroft-Nowicki system.

The claims Ryall made in her book about her traditional pre-Gardnerian form of Wicca from the West Country were fairly quickly debunked by researchers and academics, most notably professor Ronald Hutton, who concluded that "in Australia, she has devised her own variety of Wicca, which she has tried here to pass off as an old tradition."[17] With this in mind, and knowing that Ryall lived and practiced geographically close to groups founded by Goodman and his contemporaries, it is more likely that the "tell stones" she described are heavily based on the Ashcroft-Nowicki system that was being taught and used by those groups at the same time that Ryall was writing her book.

Ryall's querent stone is unmarked and painted green but otherwise performs the same function as the Eye stone in Ashcroft-Nowicki's system. A stone with a gold spot and one with a silver spot have identical meanings to the Ashcroft-Nowicki

17. Hutton, *The Triumph of the Moon*, 302.

Sun and Star stones. The Moon, Rings, and Water stones are also exactly the same. The Crossed Spears, Birds, Sickle, and Harvest stones become stones bearing an even-armed cross, a gate, a door, and an apple in Ryall's system, but the divinatory meanings from the Ashcroft-Nowicki system are all retained in their entirety.[18]

1998: Susan Sheppard

In 1998, North American astrologer and author Susan Sheppard published a book called *A Witch's Runes: How to Make and Use Your Own Magick Stones*. In the book, she described a system of thirteen stones she claimed to be drawn originally from Pictish symbols but were in fact very close to the runes described by Ashcroft-Nowicki some twenty years earlier.[19]

Sheppard's system contains all ten of Ashcroft-Nowicki's runes, with the Birds stone renamed to Flight and the Crossed Spears renamed to Crossroads. It also contains three other runes: Woman, Man, and Romance. The meanings of these three runes are almost identical to the meanings of the Woman, Man, and Love runes first outlined in Corby's 1975 system.

Thirteen stones in Sheppard's system makes for some neat associations in terms of correspondences: Sheppard is an astrologer and associated every stone but the Eye with a different zodiac sign, as well as planetary correspondences. It is Sheppard's thirteen-stone system that you will see most commonly available for sale in witchy spaces online, sometimes with a fourteenth blank stone.

In 2016, Canadian author and high priestess Dr. Alexandra Chauran mentions in her book *Runes for Beginners: Simple Divination and Interpretation* the system described by Sheppard. Chauran suggests this system is one of the most suitable for beginners—or for those who have trouble memorising the symbols in more complicated divinatory systems such as tarot.[20]

2001: Kate West

The set of eight Witches' Runes that closely resembles Crowther's is also mentioned by United Kingdom author and high priestess Kate West, first in her book *The Real Witches' Handbook: A Complete Introduction to the Craft*, published

18. Ryall, *West Country Wicca*, 85–86.
19. Sheppard, *A Witch's Runes*, 5.
20. Chauran, *Runes for Beginners*, 18.

in 2001, some twenty years after Crowther wrote about them.[21] West described this set in more detail in her 2003 book *The Real Witches' Book of Spells and Rituals*. The only difference in the symbols between West's and Crowther's sets is that Crowther's Lucky stone (a variation on the earlier Wheat/Harvest stone in Ashcroft-Nowicki's article) was now a branch with leaves. What had been a curling wave on Crowther's Wave stone was now a snake, but it carried almost identical divinatory meanings to the earlier iteration of the stone.[22]

For the most part, West suggests the same colours for certain symbols—aligned with certain elements—first outlined by Crowther: gold for the Sun stone, silver for the Moon, red for the Crossed Spears, blue for the Snake/Wave, pink for the Rings, and a white symbol on black—now marked with a # rather than a capital-*H* shape—for the black stone that replaced Ashcroft-Nowicki's original Sickle stone. The only differences in the colours suggested by Crowther and those suggested by West are on the Wheat/Lucky stone (which now bears a green branch sprouting leaves) and the Birds stone, which Crowther had said should be white, red, and blue. West stipulated only white be used.[23]

Similarly to Ashcroft-Nowicki, Crowther, and Cunningham, West also suggests not bothering the stones too much with questions, going further to say that three is the maximum number of questions that should be asked in any one sitting. West shared the thinking of earlier writers about how to perform a reading, saying that the stones "nearest to you are the ones with the most immediate influence. Those near to each other influence one another, with those nearer to you having the stronger influence."[24]

2022: *Judy Ann Nock*

American musician and author Judy Ann Nock cites both Corby and Sheppard in her book *The Modern Witchcraft Guide to Runes: Your Complete Guide to the Divination Power of Runes*, though the thirteen-stone system she outlines is the same as Sheppard's, not Corby's.

Building on the work of Sheppard, Nock offers advice on spells, psychometry reading techniques, and more to use with the runes. She also likens the imagery

21. West, *The Real Witches' Handbook*.
22. West, *The Real Witches' Book of Spells and Rituals*, 153.
23. West, *The Real Witches' Book of Spells and Rituals*, 154.
24. West, *The Real Witches' Book of Spells and Rituals*, 154.

to Bronze Age carvings and ancient Egyptian hieroglyphs and implies that the symbols might once have been a way that witches kept messages and meanings secret from those who would do them harm.[25]

2024: Jennifer Heather

In her 2024 book *The Witches' Runes: A Guide to Crafting and Connecting with the Witch Stones,* United Kingdom author Jennifer Heather built upon Sheppard's system, keeping the images but making some changes to the astrological associations and also adding correspondences to Greek and Roman mythological figures for each stone.[26]

Evolution

Looking at these different systems as well as the changes over time, we can see that there are several distinct rune sets that have been passed between practitioners and evolved with use. While they have each been labelled the "Witches' Runes," there are essentially two lineages or core versions with subsequent variations. Broadly speaking, this can be divided into an American system, which can be traced back to Corby's article in the United States and Canada, and a British system, or those that are descended from Ashcroft-Nowicki's article in the United Kingdom.

The systems outlined by both Corby and Ashcroft-Nowicki lay the groundwork for countless variations of the Witches' Runes that would go on to be used all over the world. Some would be written about in books and periodicals, while others would evolve quietly over time and be shared between teachers and students in different traditions and initiatory lines, each person adding their own flavour to the way these runes look and are read. Taking this broad categorisation and grouping the various versions of the Witches' Runes along these lines, we end up with the following:

- The Corby version, which started with fourteen runes and has been expanded in different ways and into slightly different systems, mostly by authors and practitioners in North America. Systems in this lineage include those developed by Ed Fitch and Scott Cunningham.

25. Nock, *The Modern Witchcraft Guide to Runes,* 16.
26. Heather, *The Witches' Runes.*

- The Ashcroft-Nowicki version, which started with ten runes and was written about by authors—often Wiccan or adjacent to Wicca—and used by practitioners in the United Kingdom before being shared elsewhere around the world. Systems in this lineage include Patricia Crowther, Rhiannon Ryall, Susan Sheppard, Kate West, Judy Ann Nock, and Jennifer Heather.

The later American authors, from Sheppard on, have more of a hybridised system that is based in Ashcroft-Nowicki's work but incorporates aspects of Corby's set. In our experience, practitioners from the United Kingdom—especially those who learn their craft in coven-based or lineaged traditions—still tend to use the Ashcroft-Nowicki version of the runes, without the later additions by Sheppard.

With the publication of *A Witch's Runes* in 1998, Sheppard brought her version of the Ashcroft-Nowicki runes—with the addition of a few of the Corby runes—to North American audiences, and she is often credited in later texts with devising the system herself.

Which Runes Are the Right Ones?

The Witches' Runes are unique to witches. Unlike many other divinatory rune systems, they are not based on or borrowed from an ancient alphabet or symbolism. They are used purely for divination and were created for that purpose. As we've discussed in this chapter, they have evolved over time, and the practitioners who have used them have made their own mark on them, meaning there are numerous different versions and interpretations out there. Depending on how you learn the runes and who teaches them to you, the lore around how to cast, read, and interpret them can vary.

Which system is the most accurate and authentic and wise? There isn't one answer. There can't be. Throughout the last hundred years, and especially before the coming of the internet, knowledge was passed on through teachers and books, at festivals, and through community. The knowledge being shared was coloured by those passing it on, by those who passed on what *they* learned, and so on. This is still the case in in-person groups and covens. Modern witchcraft as a whole is—and should be—a living tradition, as vibrant and varied as the people who work it.

The system we write about in this book is largely similar to the Ashcroft-Nowicki runes. The lore we have learned and passed on in writing this book is what we have been taught by those who had that lore passed on to them. We have also added some of our own insights, which we've gathered as we've worked with the runes over time.

Chapter Two

MEETING THE WITCHES' RUNES

The language of the Witches' Runes hums with timeless energy, woven into the fabric of the earth, the wind, the stars, and the bones of those who listen. As we step onto the path of the witch, these symbols become more than mere marks on stone or wood—they become living gateways to hidden wisdom. The runes carry the whispers of the ancestors, the songs of the elements, and the untamed pulse of the natural world.

In this chapter, you will read about each rune individually, as well as how they function as a set. These are not the runes of kings and warriors but the runes of the witch: symbols of transformation, divination, and motion. As we throw them—usually by dropping them and reading those that show their faces to us—they can guide us through the cycles of life and death, through the mysteries of creation and destruction, and offer a mirror to our own unfolding power.

Each rune holds its own voice, ready to speak through the lapping of waves or the silence of the moon on a clear night. We will not simply study their meanings; we will enter into dialogue with the runes themselves, learning to hear their call and feel their resonance within us. It is through this process of listening that we begin to unlock their secrets—not through pure intellect but through our own intuitions, practices, and connections to the symbols and spirits of the runes.

To meet the runes is to invite them into our lives, to see them as allies in our work as witches. They offer guidance and insight in times of uncertainty, reveal hidden truths, and awaken parts of us that we may not yet be aware of. Through their simple symbols, we deepen our bond with the mysteries of magic and our own minds, learning to navigate life and the unseen with clarity, purpose, and trust. Prepare to meet the runes not as a distant concept but as companions on your journey—each one an invitation to explore the layers of magic and self.

The Runes as a Set

The Witches' Runes form a circle of symbols. Each one is distinct, yet they are woven together through the threads of magic and nature. When meeting the runes as a set, we begin to experience their collective rhythms. Each one speaks to a different aspect of the craft and life, while together they form a larger harmonious whole.

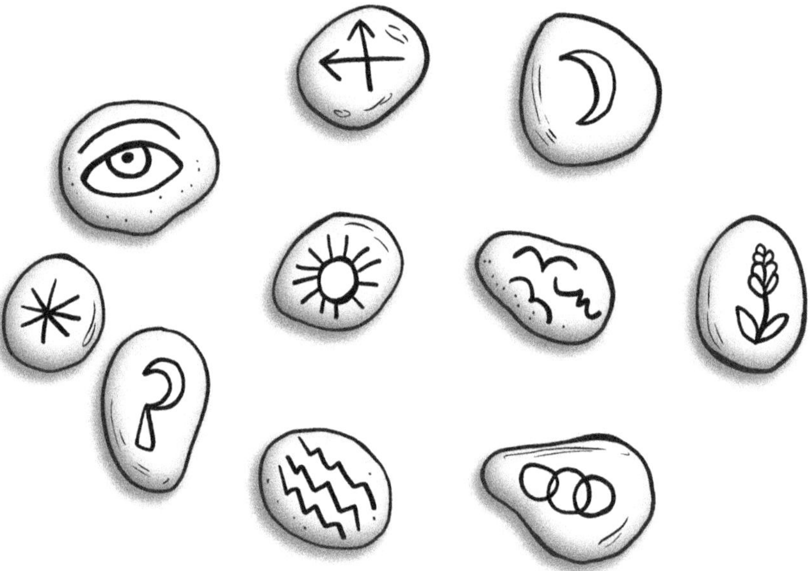

The individual meanings of the runes are listed in the coming pages, but take care to think of them as parts of a whole rather than discrete, isolated units. Together, these ten runes form a living breathing system. They interact, shift, and evolve, offering insight and guidance for those who walk the path of the witch. When read as a set, they weave a story, each rune adding a layer to the unfolding narrative, showing us how the energies of life, nature, and spirit intertwine.

This is perhaps one of the more complex layers of this divination set. Quite apart from having precise and unchanging meaning, they work in relationship to each other—with nuanced meanings emerging from their interactions within a given reading. This is not a static process or a subject for rote learning: this system is built of relationships and includes your own relationship to the runes. This is worth taking into consideration when you begin the process of making your own set.

Performing a Reading with the Witches' Runes

The following basic instructions provide a foundational approach to using the Witches' Runes for insight. A more detailed guide on divination techniques, including more elaborate methods of interpretation, can be found in chapter 14.

1. *Formulate Your Question:* Begin by clearly formulating your question. This can be a specific inquiry or a broader request for insight. The more precise the question, the clearer the response will be.
2. *Prepare the Runes:* Gather the stones in your hands, holding them lightly. Take a moment to focus on your intention, allowing yourself to connect with the energy of the runes.
3. *Wake Up the Runes:* Blow gently on the stones, infusing them with your breath. This act symbolises your intent and the transfer of your question to the runes.
4. *Shake and Cast:* Shake the runes within your hands, mixing them while keeping your focus on the question. When you feel ready, toss them onto a flat surface.
5. *Interpret the Layout:* Only consider the runes that land face up. Any that land face down are ignored for this reading, as they are not currently offering insight. Observe their positioning: Runes that fall close together may be influencing each other, while isolated runes may hold singular importance. There is more information about combinations in chapter 14. Consider the meaning of each rune in relation to the question asked and the way they interact with one another.
6. *Reflect on the Message:* Take a moment to reflect on the reading as a whole. What themes emerge? How do the runes relate to your current situation? Use intuition alongside established meanings to deepen your understanding.

The Individual Runes

Each rune has an individual tone from which the interactions and interpretations will be built. The essence of each rune is intuitive in its meaning. You might find the individual ideas simplistic, but they are meant to serve as guideposts for your own connections to each rune. This will be explored in greater depth in the subsequent chapters dealing with each rune individually.

The Eye Rune

The Eye represents the querent, the signifier. When interpreted like this, the Eye stone is placed face up at the start of a reading. It can also symbolise the act of seeing and being seen and can indicate what is known, what is hidden, and what is in focus.

Keywords: Signifier, perception, awareness, intuition, wisdom, revelation, clairvoyance, discernment, truth-seeing, secrets revealed, inner vision.

The Sun Rune

The Sun represents vitality, illumination, and the transformative power of light, symbolising growth, clarity, and the expression of life force. It can also reflect the idea of enlightenment and creative power, offering insight and strength in both spiritual and material realms. Crowther claimed that having the Sun as the "leading" stone in a reading (i.e., having it the closest stone to the Eye) was a sign of a successful year ahead.[27] When it appears near the Wheat stone, the Sun usually signals the birth of something new.

Keywords: Strength, growth, positive aspects, energy, fruitfulness.

The Moon Rune

The Moon represents intuition, mystery, and the subconscious. It is often linked to dreams, cycles, and hidden influences. It encourages trust in one's inner voice while acknowledging the presence of illusions,

---

27. Crowther, *Lid Off the Cauldron*, 111.

emotions, and unseen forces at play. Ashcroft-Nowicki related this stone to feminine energy and the querent's personality.[28]

Keywords: Clouded vision, something hidden, outside of one's awareness, dreams, the Otherworld, intuition.

The Rings Rune

The Rings often signifies relationships, agreements, and the ways in which things come together to form something greater. In this way, it can also relate to responsibilities that come with commitments. Crowther surmised that the combination of the Rings and the Waves pointed to a romance that would take the querent abroad.[29]

Keywords: Union, connection, commitment, contracts, partnerships, patterns, obligations, interdependence, binding forces, creation through unity.

The Birds Rune

The Birds represents communication, movement, and messages, often signalling news, omens, or the need for clarity in expression. It can indicate swift changes, gossip, or the influence of external voices, urging discernment in what is heard and spoken.

Keywords: Messages, unexpected news, communication, children, journeys, travel.

The Waves Rune

The Waves rune embodies the constant motion of life, symbolising change, fluidity, and the cycles of nature and emotion. It represents the power of intuition, adaptability, and the harmonious flow of energy, urging one to embrace life's ebb and flow with grace. Alongside the Moon, this stone sometimes points to an accident or illness. The Waves stone falling near the Star is often interpreted as foretelling the birth of a child in or around the querent's family.

Keywords: High emotions, fluid situations, the Underworld.

---

28. Ashcroft-Nowicki, "The Gypsy Runes," 235.
29. Crowther, *Lid Off the Cauldron*, 112.

The Wheat Rune

The Wheat rune signifies abundance, fertility, and growth, symbolising the cycle of life, nourishment, and harvest. It represents the fruitful results of patience, effort, and perseverance, highlighting the connection between the physical and spiritual realms through sustenance and renewal. Goodman wrote that the combination of the Wheat rune and the Rings often speaks to a business partnership.[30] If the Rings and the Wheat are present in a reading with three or more stones other than the main Eye stone, it is often a sign that the entire reading is for the querent's family rather than the querent.

Keywords: Harvest, profit, the rewards of hard work—especially physical work, endings, climax.

The Crossed Spears Rune

The Crossed Spears rune symbolises conflict, challenge, and confrontation, representing both external struggles and internal tensions. It can indicate a need for strategy, courage, or resolution, urging the seeker to face obstacles with determination and clarity. Alongside the Sickle, this indicates a serious argument or falling out.

Keywords: Conflict, discord, unrest, clashing energies, heated parting words.

The Star Rune

The Star symbolises guidance, inspiration, and destiny, representing hope and a sense of higher purpose. It encourages trust in one's path, illuminating the way forward and revealing opportunities for growth and fulfilment. When the Sun and the Star land near each other, they represent the querent's hopes and dreams, but these hopes and dreams will go unfulfilled if the Moon is present without the Sun.

Keywords: Ambitions, ideals, energy, inspiration, hope, seeing clearly.

---

30. Goodman, "Stones O'Leary."

The Sickle Rune

The Sickle represents endings, harvest, and necessary separation, symbolising the act of cutting away what no longer serves. It signifies both loss and liberation, urging decisive action to clear the path for new growth. When present near the Waves, it often points to a physical parting, of someone moving away.

Keywords: Death, monumental change, an abrupt and drastic ending.

Creating Your Rune Set

These days, you can purchase your own set of Witches' Runes fairly easily—just as you would a tarot deck. If this is what you want to do, go for it! But we recommend creating your own set, getting to know each stone in turn as you do. By crafting your own set, you will end up with a divinatory system that is uniquely yours and with which you will likely resonate with more than something you have purchased.

The next ten chapters will explore the deeper meanings of each rune and will also walk you through creating your own set. At this point, it's best to focus on the process rather than on accumulating stones. We've also included a consecration ritual, which can be used to set your intention to use the stones and to dedicate them to your practice.

Most of the sources we've looked at and the lore we received in our own training focuses on the Witches' Runes being drawn, painted, or etched onto actual stones, usually collected by the reader themselves. But it is possible to create sets of runes from wooden disks, sticks, bones, gemstones, or any material you might make other rune sets with.

Selecting Your Stones

Choosing the stones for your rune set is a subtle process that begins with presence and patience. You might collect all your stones at once or individually, each time seeking out a specific stone that you feel fits its intended symbol. Keep in mind that the stones should be big and flat enough to incorporate the images, and as a set, they should be small enough to fit into your cupped hands. Don't rush this process, and let it unfold. It is better to take the time to find the right stones than to quickly find a set of stones you don't enjoy.

Rather than selecting stones purely for their appearance, our approach invites you to look beyond the surface, to let each stone speak to you in its own way. Try the following when you encounter a stone that catches your eye or you think might work for your rune set—or any other magic for that matter: Hold the stone in your hand, feeling its weight, texture, and shape. Close your eyes and let your attention settle into your heart. In this stillness, ask if the stone is meant to be part of this journey. Listen closely—not only to what you hear but to what you feel.

If you sense a clear yes—a warmth, a pull, a feeling that this is right—then you've likely found a stone that's aligned with this work. If you receive no impression or feel a subtle (or not-so-subtle) no, trust that as well. This stone may be perfect for something else but is not meant for this particular purpose. Remember that stones have been going about their business for a long time and not all of them will fit with you. There's no rush. Take your time with each choice, trusting that the right stones will reveal themselves.

As you go through this process, you may find that each stone brings its own presence, a unique energy that will contribute to the final set. Some may have the feel of ancient wisdom, while others might be lighter, perhaps bringing clarity or grounding. When you've gathered stones that feel aligned, know that you've begun the work of cocreating a tool for exploration, insight, and connection. Each stone is now a chosen part of this project, ready to be transformed with your intention and artistry.

Here are more quick tips, lore, and common sense concerning the selection and creation of your runes.

Using Sea Stones versus Earth Stones

In the Ashcroft-Nowicki article, she mentions "sea stones" and "earth stones." She was taught to collect and use sea stones because, she said, the woman who trained her, Vashti, recognised in her an affinity with the sea due to her home in the Channel Islands.[31] It is the sea stones' lore that has carried through most of the sets inspired or passed "downstream" from Ashcroft-Nowicki's original set. There doesn't appear to be much written anywhere about "Kerry" or earth stones.

31. Ashcroft-Nowicki, "The Gypsy Runes."

Collecting Stones from Waterways

Ashcroft-Nowicki said in her original article that sea stones are best collected during the ebbing tide, ideally during spring tides or after autumn storms.[32] In our time working with and teaching this system, we have discovered stones collected from rivers, creeks, and lakes also work well.

Collecting Stones from Other Natural Places

If your plan is to collect what Ashcroft-Nowicki calls Kerry stones—earth stones—these should be collected "at a time of day which is neither light nor dark" and ideally from just below the Earth's surface.[33]

When collecting stones from anywhere in nature, it's important to be mindful of local laws around removing natural material. In Australia, for example, these laws vary from state to state, and in the case of some national and state parks, laws are there to protect culturally or ecologically significant areas.

Using Store-Bought Stones

If your location or circumstances prevent you from seeking out and collecting your stones, you could purchase your own. Many hardware stores sell tumbled river stones as an accessory for terrariums and fish tanks.

Choosing Shape and Size

As we mentioned earlier, the size of your stones is really up to you, as long as you can hold them as a set in your two cupped hands. The original article stipulated they should be "well shaped," which means they should be able to fall flat on two sides.[34] They should also be a colour and texture suitable to be painted or drawn upon, if that is how you intend to mark them.

Marking Your Stones

The markings on the stones should be simple ones. There are many paints and markers available for sale these days that will work on stone. If you are painting or drawing the images onto the stones, consider finishing them with a clear

---

32. Ashcroft-Nowicki, "The Gypsy Runes," 235.
33. Ashcroft-Nowicki, "The Gypsy Runes," 233.
34. Ashcroft-Nowicki, "The Gypsy Runes," 235.

sealant coat to prevent the images from rubbing or scratching off. There are also smaller handheld engraving tools on the market that are relatively simple to use; just be sure to follow the safety instructions around these tools and the potentially hazardous dust they produce.

Taking Your Time

Take care to feel out each stone as you handle it. The right stone for the right symbol will usually make itself known to you in time. You can collect one stone at a time and build your relationship with that rune while waiting for the rest of your set to find you. The process in this book will help you to build your set. Even if you find all of your stones in quick succession, we advise you to take the time to work with each stone individually to ensure a depth of understanding and a personal connection to each rune.

Ritual: Consecrating and Cleansing Your Stones

Certain magical traditions hold that natural items do not require magical consecration or cleansing. You might find that working with local spirits to find your set of stones and then completing the exercises in later chapters is enough to create a magically and personally powerful rune set. It is ultimately up to the individual practitioner to decide which approach is most appropriate for them.

Seeking, choosing, then creating a set of these stones is an act of consecration in and of itself. If you bought your stones, or if you do feel the need to consecrate your set, you could try the following short ritual:

Materials Needed

- A small bowl of water (water element; preferably spring or blessed water)
- Incense for purification (air or fire element, depending on witchcraft tradition). If you can obtain a resin incense such as frankincense, or "church incense," to burn on a briquet, do so. If not, sandalwood is also a great choice for elevating a space.
- Salt (earth element)
- A white taper candle (You can use pillar or tealight candles in a pinch.)

- Your complete set of painted or etched Witches' Runes
- A cloth or pouch to place the runes in after consecration
- A lighter or matches

Directions

1. ***Cast the Circle:*** Begin by creating sacred space. Light the candle and incense, and visualise a protective circle around you, calling upon the four elements or your deities/spirits to guard the ritual.
2. ***Elemental Cleansing with Water:*** Take the bowl of water and sprinkle it lightly over the rune set, saying: *With water, I cleanse these stones of all negativity, washing them clean of all that does not serve.*
3. ***Elemental Cleansing with Fire (Incense):*** Pass each rune through the incense smoke, saying: *With the power of fire, I purify and awaken the spirit within each rune.*
4. ***Elemental Cleansing with Earth (Salt):*** Sprinkle a small amount of salt over the stones or lightly rub each rune with a bit of salt, saying: *By earth, I ground and connect these runes to the ancient wisdom of the land.*
5. ***Elemental Cleansing with Air (Incense Smoke or Breath):*** Hold each rune and either blow on it gently or pass it through the incense again, saying: *By air, I breathe life into these symbols, that they may speak with clarity and truth.*
6. ***Consecration:*** Hold your hands over the set of runes and say:

I consecrate these runes in the name of the Old Ones,
By the powers of earth, air, fire, and water,
By the light of the sun and the mystery of the moon.
May these stones serve as vessels of wisdom and magic,
Speaking true when called upon.
I charge you to work only in alignment with my highest good
And the highest good of all.
So mote it be.

7. ***Charging:*** Place the runes in the light of the candle. You may sit in meditation for a few moments, focusing on imbuing the runes with your intention. Visualise light filling each rune with energy and purpose.

8. ***Close the Circle:*** Once you feel the ritual is complete, thank the elements and any deities or spirits you've invoked, then close the circle by visualising the energy receding back into the earth.

Your rune set is now cleansed, consecrated, and ready for use. Store the stones in a cloth or pouch and keep them in a sacred space when not in use.

If you ever feel that your stones need cleansing, simply hold them under running water for a minute or two. Or, better yet, take them to a beach or other body of water and let natural water rush over them.

Storing Your Stones

Ashcroft-Nowicki mentions in her article that she stores her stones in a chamois leather pouch.[35] Most folks we have come across who work with these stones store theirs in a simple cloth or leather pouch or bag, or in a small box. You can make a pouch of your own by stitching together two rectangles of cloth and leaving one short side open. Turn the pouch out the right way so the seams are inside, then put a drawstring in the top or simply tie it closed.

Time to Meet the Stones

By now, you should have a rough idea of the images on the ten stones and maybe some inklings as to how they might be interpreted in a reading. Over the next ten chapters, we will walk you through some of the deeper and more nuanced associations with each stone and prepare you to create a set of stones with which you will have a meaningful affinity—a set of stones that will speak to you.

---

35. Ashcroft-Nowicki, "The Gypsy Runes," 237.

Chapter Three
The Eye Stone

The Eye stone represents the querent, Odin's eye given for knowledge. It depicts a single human eye, usually lidded or with eyelashes, looking either straight ahead or off to the side. Where it has been drawn looking off to one side, a reader could use its line of sight to determine the querent's current focus or follow the Eye's gaze at the stones opposite to these to figure out what's been neglected or overlooked in the querent's life.

In many rune sets, the Eye stone is often slightly bigger or flatter than the other nine. Sometimes it is an oval-ish shape. This could be something to look for when collecting your Eye stone. It makes sense that this stone would be the most prominent in a set, as it represents the querent: It is often placed in front of the reader before the other stones are cast, to denote the centre point of the reading. Those who toss the Eye stone along with the others tend to use the second description, interpreting it as symbolising perception or knowledge when it appears in a reading alongside other stones.

In a Reading

This rune is distinctive in that it offers two possible interpretations in a reading: the focal point or perception.

The first approach is to treat it as a focal point: the centre from which the significance or timing of other runes is measured. In this sense, the Eye represents the "I" of the reading. Wherever it appears, the runes closest to it hold the greatest importance or exert the strongest influence. Some readers interpret this spatial proximity as a reflection of time, with nearer runes indicating events closer in time and distant placements representing far-off events. It is also possible to assume a degree of probability in this way, with distant runes having more potential for circumvention or alteration due to the impact of the way closer events unfold.

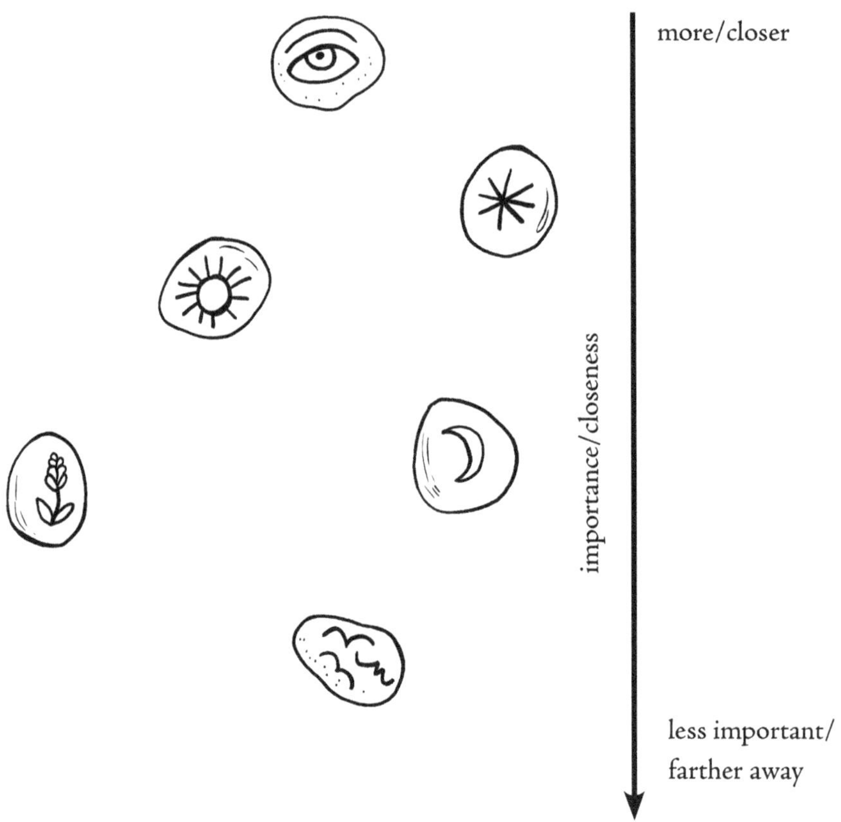

The second approach views the rune as a symbol of perception. Here, it can reveal what is currently occupying the querent's attention or, conversely, what is distracting them. When framed this way, the rune may also indicate what lies ahead for the querent on their path rather than what is behind them.

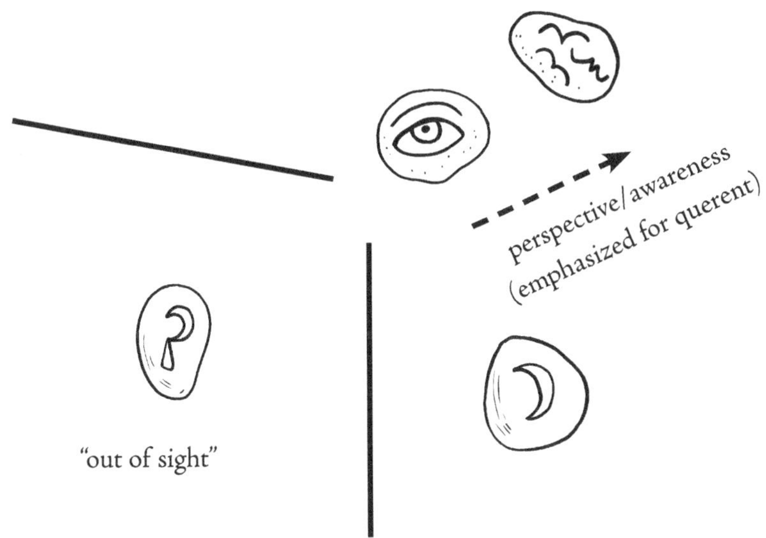

In Culture and Mythology

The eye as a symbol has attracted rich mythological associations and symbolic meanings throughout recorded history. Across various stories, recurring themes emerge: the protective power of a watcher or guardian, the connection between vision and wisdom, and the often-high cost of knowledge. These references may shape or deepen your interpretation of this rune. Feel free to explore these concepts further, drawing on the exercises for inspiration. Here are some examples of the eye as a symbol in myth and story to inspire you.

The Eye of Horus

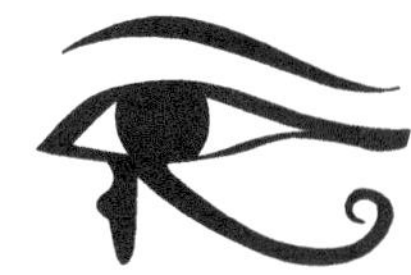

One of the most iconic eye motifs, the Eye of Horus originates from the myth of Set's rebellion and the murder of Osiris in ancient Egyptian mythology. In this tale, Horus loses an eye in battle with his uncle Set, though it is later restored when he triumphs. He sacrifices this eye as an offering to his father, Osiris. This act revives Osiris in the afterlife and restores harmony to the cosmos. The Eye of Horus has since come to symbolise healing and protection, especially in funerary contexts. Horus, the falcon-headed sky deity, was believed to have eyes representing the sun and the moon.[36] Some Egyptologists, such as Richard Wilkinson and Rolf Krauss, link the symbol to the phases of the moon, which mirror the eye's loss and recovery; however, there is contention around when this correlation developed.[37]

The Graeae

From Greek mythology, the Graeae are three sisters—Deino, Enyo, and Pemphredo—daughters of sea deities and siblings of the Gorgons. They are often described as ancient, though Hesiod calls them fair cheeked in *Theogony*, and Aeschylus claimed them to be swan shaped in *Prometheus Bound*. Most notably, they share a single eye, which allows them to see all things, though their visions often skew toward the dark or foreboding, such as the manner of one's death.[38] This reflects the idea that ignorance is bliss and symbolises the price of knowledge.

The Evil Eye Bead

The eye motif is a long-standing amulet used to ward off the evil eye and malefic forces, particularly in Mediterranean and Near Eastern cultures. Known by various names, including *mati* in Greece and *nazar* in Turkey, the amulet is typically crafted from blue glass and worn as jewellery or hung as a protective ornament.[39] Theories of its function vary. Some believe it works through the principle of like attracting like, drawing a curse to the eye and away from its intended target, while others see it as a form of spiritual surveillance. It is also said that the bead will break when it has absorbed a curse, signalling its need to be replaced.

Odin's Eye

In Norse mythology, Odin's relentless pursuit of wisdom led him to make a great sacrifice—one that forever altered his perception of the world. He journeyed to Mimir's Well, a sacred source of knowledge hidden beneath the roots of

---

36. Krauss, "The Eye of Horus and the Planet Venus," 193–208.
37. Wilkinson, *Reading Egyptian*, 43, 83.
38. Roman and Roman, *Encyclopedia of Greek and Roman Mythology*, 181.
39. Williams, *Celebrating Life Customs Around the World*, 344.

Yggdrasil, the World Tree. Mimir, the well's guardian, demanded a high price for a single draught from its waters: Odin's eye. Without hesitation, Odin plucked out his own eye and cast it into the well, gaining not just knowledge but a profound shift in awareness.

This act of self-sacrifice can be interpreted as more than just a transaction for wisdom. In giving up an eye, Odin was not merely losing sight but transforming his vision. One eye remained fixed on the physical world, while the other became attuned to the hidden realms beyond the veil. His ability to see into the unseen, to grasp the deeper truths of existence, was born from this exchange. This dual sight—one in the world of men, the other in the world of spirits—reinforces his role as a god of wisdom, magic, and prophecy.

Odin's story speaks to the nature of initiation and the cost of enlightenment. True knowledge is rarely gained without sacrifice, and once acquired, it alters us forever. As Oliver Wendell Holmes famously observed in *The Autocrat of the Breakfast-Table*, "A man's mind, once stretched by a new idea, never returns to its original dimensions."[40] Odin's sacrifice reflects this truth—he was never the same after drinking from Mimir's Well. His wandering nature and close ties to ravens, wolves, and other spirit allies further suggest that his wisdom was not static but ever growing, shaped by experience and the mysteries he sought to unravel.

In many ways, Odin's sacrifice echoes the Hermetic principle that perception shapes reality. His willingness to surrender one form of sight in exchange for another suggests that knowledge is not simply about acquiring information but about changing the way we see and engage with the world. His story invites us to consider what we might be willing to sacrifice in the pursuit of deeper understanding—and whether we are prepared for the transformation that wisdom inevitably brings.

Argus Panoptes

In Greek mythology, Argus Panoptes is a giant who was given the name of "All-Seeing," a fitting title for one blessed with a hundred eyes. As a loyal servant of the goddess Hera, he was assigned the task of guarding Io, a nymph Zeus had transformed into a white heifer to hide their affair. Argus, with his multitude of

40. Holmes, *The Autocrat of the Breakfast-Table*, 256.

ever-watchful eyes, was the perfect warden. While some of his eyes would rest, others remained open, ensuring that nothing escaped his gaze.

Hera's choice of Argus as Io's guardian reflected not just his extraordinary sight but also his role as an enforcer of divine order. He was relentless in his duty, standing as an embodiment of constant vigilance. However, Zeus, unwilling to let Io remain under Argus's watchful eye, sent Hermes to free her. The trickster god lulled Argus into a deep sleep with music and storytelling before striking him down.

Though Argus met his end at Hermes's hand, Hera ensured that his legacy would live on. She gathered his many eyes and placed them upon the tail feathers of the peacock, one of her sacred animals. In this way, Argus's sight was never truly lost. His watchfulness became immortal, woven into the patterns of nature itself. The peacock's iridescent feathers, each marked with an eye-like design, serve as a reminder of Argus's endless vigilance, preserving his presence in the world long after his demise.

In Action

To get in touch with the Eye rune on an experiential level, spend time fully engrossed in your sense of vision.

Bring Your Awareness to Your Sight

Try it for a full day. Bring your awareness to what you can see and really get lost in the details: the grain of paper, the patterns in wood, the shades of colours, and the gradients of lighting. Really notice the way things look. How does this impact how you feel, how you perceive things, and how you think through the course of the day? If your awareness falls from this activity during the day, gently bring your focus back to it when it comes to mind. There is no judgement here. You can also schedule several periods of focused attention on your sight throughout the day.

See with Your Eyes Closed

A secondary exercise is to meditate on your vision with your eyes closed. What do you see in the darkness? How does this vision differ from the outward-looking sight explored above? Does contemplation of this internal sight have a different impact on your thoughts, emotions, and body?

Make Your Own Eye Stone

Once you have spent some time reflecting on the symbolism of the eyes or sight in mythology and tried the previous exercises, begin the process of selecting a stone that you think will suit the Eye rune. Remember that you want the full set of stones to fit comfortably in your hands in order to perform a reading, so the individual stone you collect shouldn't be unwieldy. You might have one already or have your own methods for finding one. If you need guidance here, you can review the "Selecting Your Stones" section of the previous chapter. It is helpful to hold your intention, as well as your understanding of eye symbolism, clearly in mind while you undertake this process of searching.

When you have found a stone that you think will work, carry it on your person for at least a week to build a bond and ensure that it is the right choice for this rune. Respectfully return it to where you found it if you decide it is not the one.

You might like to hold your stone while you perform the remainder of the exercises in this chapter, though this is not essential. Jason prefers to have the stone for the guided journey exercises as it brings something of the specific material into that experience. If the stone is taking a long time to locate, you might try the rest of the exercises as you search. You could also perform the guided meditation and bring your intention to find the right stone on that journey, asking the spirit of the rune for assistance.

If you do decide to proceed with the exercises and meditations without the stone, you can use a hand-drawn image of the rune as a visual aid and focus. If you use the paper option, treat it as if it were the rune stone and do not let yourself be deterred by any concerns about it being less effective.

In Thought

Observe the image of the Eye stone earlier in this chapter. Look at it until you can hold it clearly in your mind. Take the time to really get familiar with the image. When you can conjure it clearly while your eyes are closed, you are ready to proceed to the meditations. The first meditation will focus on allowing the symbol to speak to you through mental impressions. The second meditation is a guided meditation to bring you into contact with the spirit of the rune itself.

Meditation 1: Exploring the Eye Stone

The following meditation is unscripted and will help you build a connection with the image of the rune. The objective is to notice any existing concepts or associations that this rune might hold for you. By performing this exercise, you will be able to witness those ideas bubbling to the surface. Take note of anything that comes up and remember there is no right or wrong here. Spend some time recording anything that comes up in your journal when you are done.

Get into a comfortable position. Only lie down if you are able to relax without falling asleep. Whatever position you choose, ensure that your back is straight and supported.

Close your eyes and take several calming breaths. Take a moment here to check in with your body and to relax any spots where you feel tension. Let your breath dissolve and carry away any stress as your body grows soft and relaxed. Spend a minute or two here to settle into the exercise and set the intention to explore the symbol of this rune.

Now, with your eyes still closed, see the symbol of the Eye. See it as clearly as you can, holding it in your imagination. You do not have to do anything else; simply regard the symbol and be open to insights. Take note of anything that comes up for you during this time. What thoughts, concepts, or memories bubble up? Are there particular ideas that come to you? Body sensations? Take note of these things while letting your attention remain resting gently on the symbol of the Eye.

If you happen to notice that your focus has wandered away to something else, tenderly bring your attention back to the symbol. Try to remain in this meditation for at least ten minutes.

You might like to perform this meditation several times as you work with this rune. You can also revisit it periodically to integrate new insights as your relationship grows.

Meditation 2: Meeting the Spirit of the Eye Rune

This is a more in-depth meditation. The objective here is to go on a journey to meet the spirit of the Eye rune so that you can build a relationship with it. This has two secondary benefits: The first is the ability to learn directly from the rune spirit and the second is to anchor that spirit in your rune stone. You might like to record this script and play it back, perhaps with some calming music, or otherwise memorise the steps and walk yourself through them. If you record it, be sure to leave adequate time at the marked pauses for interactions and input from beings within the meditation.

Begin by finding a comfortable position and closing your eyes. Take several deep, calming breaths, and let your body relax.

Take a deep breath in… and as you exhale, let go of any tension in your body. Allow yourself to settle into this moment, leaving behind any distractions or concerns. With each breath, feel yourself becoming more relaxed, more at ease.

Now, imagine yourself standing in a beautiful forest. The air is cool and fresh, and the sound of leaves rustling in the gentle breeze surrounds you. Sunlight filters through the canopy above, casting a soft dappled light onto the forest floor.

Take a moment to feel the soil beneath your feet. The earth is solid, grounding you. Each breath you take connects you more deeply with this peaceful place.

As you walk through the forest, you notice a large, ancient tree ahead of you. Its trunk is wide and strong, its bark thick and textured. There's something magical about this tree—it's as though it has been standing here for centuries, watching over the forest.

You feel drawn to the tree. As you get closer, you notice something remarkable: There is a doorway in the trunk of the tree. It's small and rounded, just large enough for you to step through. The door itself is made of smooth wood, with intricate carvings that seem to shimmer slightly in the sunlight.

Take a moment to observe this doorway. What does it look like? Notice the details, the carvings, the way it feels as you gently reach out and touch it.

Now, when you're ready, place your hand on the door's handle. It opens easily, inviting you to step inside. Take a deep breath, and with your next exhale, step through the doorway.

As you pass through, you enter a new space. This place is calm and safe, a sanctuary just for you. Perhaps it's a beautiful garden, a peaceful meadow, or a cosy room—whatever feels right to you. Take a moment to explore this space. Feel the peace that surrounds you. You are safe here, and everything you need is already within you.

Breathe in deeply and let yourself relax even further. In this place, you are free from any worries or stress. Feel the calm washing over you, nurturing and restoring your mind and body.

Take some time here, in this space of peace and tranquillity. You can return to this place anytime you wish, simply by stepping through the doorway in the tree.

Now that you've spent some time in this tranquil place, you begin to notice something different, something new. As you explore this space—whether it's a garden, meadow, or room—you see a symbol before you. It is the shape of an eye, ancient and powerful, glowing softly in the air or etched upon a stone.

This is the Eye rune. Its presence feels important, as though it holds deep wisdom and insight. Take a moment to observe this symbol. What does it look like to you? Is it large or small? Bright or subtle? Notice its shape, its energy, and how it makes you feel.

The Eye rune represents vision, perception, and the ability to see beyond the surface. It invites you to look inward, to see clearly not only with your physical eyes but with your inner sight—the sight of your intuition, your wisdom.

Take a deep breath, and as you exhale, let yourself draw closer to the Eye rune. You feel a gentle pull towards it, as though it is calling you, inviting you to learn from it. You sense the presence of a spirit—a guide connected to the rune. This is the spirit of the Eye rune, a wise and benevolent being here to share its knowledge with you.

You feel the spirit's presence drawing nearer. It may take the form of a glowing light, a figure, or a being that feels right to you. There is no need to force an image; simply allow whatever form the spirit takes to appear naturally.

The spirit of the Eye rune greets you warmly, its energy radiating calm and wisdom. It speaks to you, though perhaps not with words but with feelings, symbols, or impressions. It communicates through the language of your heart and soul.

Take a moment to connect with this spirit. Feel the energy it brings—an energy of clarity, truth, and insight.

The spirit offers you the gift of seeing clearly—of understanding things from a new perspective. Perhaps there is a situation in your life that you seek guidance on. Or maybe there is something within yourself that you wish to understand more deeply. You feel the Eye rune's power enhancing your inner vision, opening your mind to greater wisdom and appreciation.

The spirit of the Eye rune invites you to ask a question. You may ask about your life, your path, or anything that feels important to you at this moment. When you are ready, silently or aloud, ask your question.

(Pause for reflection, to connect and receive guidance.)

The spirit responds not with direct answers but with symbols, images, or a deep sense of knowing. Trust what you receive, even if it feels subtle or abstract. The Eye rune teaches us to see beyond what is obvious—to perceive the hidden truths and deeper meaning.

Take a moment to sit with this wisdom. Know that whatever guidance you have received is for your highest good, and you can return to this space and this spirit whenever you seek clarity or insight.

Now, the spirit of the Eye rune offers you a final message—something simple yet profound that you can carry with you into your waking life. Listen closely, and when you are ready, receive this message with an open heart.

(Pause briefly to receive the message.)

As your time with the spirit of the Eye rune comes to an end, you feel a sense of gratitude. The spirit slowly begins to fade, leaving behind the powerful symbol of the Eye rune, still glowing softly in the space around you.

Take a deep breath, knowing that the wisdom you've gained here will stay with you, guiding you even as you return to the present.

When you are ready, turn away from the rune and begin to walk back towards the doorway in the tree. Feel the peacefulness of this place and know that you can always return to seek more guidance when you need it.

Step through the doorway once more, returning to the forest. Feel the ground beneath your feet, hear the soft rustling of the leaves, and sense the calm of nature around you.

With each breath, bring yourself back to the present moment. Begin to notice your body again, feeling your fingers and toes, the surface beneath you.

When you are ready, gently open your eyes, carrying with you the insight and wisdom of the Eye rune.

When you have finished, take a moment to record your insights: What did you see? What have you learnt? Did anything surprise you? As part of your records, you can sketch out any particularly vivid imagery that came through your meditation as a way of grounding it into the physical world.

You might also like to try a grounding exercise to help bring you back to the present moment. This can be achieved by standing barefoot on the earth, imagining energetic roots reaching from your feet into the ground and balancing your energy, or resting your forehead on the floor for a moment.

In Words

Take the time to journal your thoughts and experiences. Reflect on the ideas raised in this section. Are there particular concepts that resonate with you or you find particularly repellent? Explore these feelings and any reasons you think might lay behind them.

Consider the myths you explored—did any particular story resonate with you more than the others? If so, reflect on why it captured your attention. Perhaps it evoked a personal connection, revealed a new perspective, or deepened your understanding of the rune's symbolism.

Take a moment to think about the role of vision, both physically and spiritually. How do these two forms of sight compare? Is vision purely about perceiving the physical world, or does it extend beyond that—into intuition, insight, or the ability to see truth beyond appearances? Consider how this relates to your own experiences and how you engage with the world around you.

As you work through the meditation exercises, record your impressions. What sensations arose? Did any images, emotions, or messages come through? These reflections will help you track your progress and refine your understanding of the rune over time.

Finally, without looking at your notes, write out your own interpretation of the stone and what it represents to you. Let your thoughts flow naturally, drawing on your direct experiences rather than relying on written references. This exercise can reveal what has truly settled into your understanding and highlight any areas you might want to explore further.

Chapter Four
THE SUN STONE

The sun on the Sun stone is usually represented by a simple circle with single lines as the rays. The radiant, blazing sun may be simply drawn, but its divinatory meanings are powerful and positive. Often representing wealth, happiness, and prosperity, this rune has a favourable influence on the meanings of those around it. It might signal a happy ending or satisfying conclusion to an ongoing issue, or simply a turn of the tide and the light at the end of the tunnel for a situation that had hitherto seemed almost hopeless.

In our time using and teaching this system, we've made or come across sets where the Sun is sometimes on a stone lighter in colour than the rest of the set or flecked with mica (fool's gold), or in a similar or complementary shape to the Moon stone. We've seen this rune burned into wood to include the element of fire in its creation or simply drawn in shiny gold marker. Crowther and later West both suggest this rune should be painted in gold paint.[41] Others choose not to include any of these distinguishing features, sticking to a simple sun on a simple stone.

In a Reading

This rune is overwhelmingly a positive presence. It can be held to represent masculine energy, but more commonly it represents wealth, happiness, and prosperity. The positive influence of this rune can imply a happy ending or successful

41. West, *The Real Witches' Book of Spells and Rituals.*

conclusion to something. It can also forecast a beneficial change in circumstances. In many ways, this rune is comparable to the Sun card in the tarot.

In Culture and Mythology

The sun has been a symbol of central importance across time and cultures. It embodies light, the seasons, and the fertility of crops. It dispels darkness and evil, heals, but also burns whatever ventures too close. Its rays are likened to the lustre of gold. As the centre of our solar system and the hour hand of our seasonal cycles, the sun occupies a pivotal role in human experience, inspiring a vast array of myths, symbols, and magical associations. We introduce you to a few here and encourage you to investigate further.

The Clear Sight of Helios

In ancient Greek mythology, Helios is more than just the personification of the sun—he is a force of revelation, truth, and unwavering vision. Each day he rides his golden chariot across the sky, pulled by his fire-breathing horses, casting light over the world and seeing all that unfolds beneath him. His presence is not merely a source of warmth and life but also of knowledge, for nothing escapes his gaze.

Helios is closely associated with oaths, truth, and divine justice. His all-seeing nature makes him an unerring witness, a being whose vision cannot be deceived. In the myth of Persephone's abduction, it is Helios alone (or in some versions of the myth, Helios and Hecate) who observes Hades seizing the young goddess and carrying her into the Underworld. As the sun, he illuminates the event, making him a source of knowledge that others must turn to when seeking hidden truths. This role of the sun as a revealer of secrets—both physical and metaphysical—deeply informs later esoteric traditions, where solar symbolism is linked to enlightenment, spiritual clarity, and the illumination of the unknown.

Helios's ability to witness all things also connects him to themes of divine judgement. To swear an oath by Helios was to place oneself under the scrutiny of an unyielding force of truth. In this way, the sun represents not just light but the moral clarity that comes with seeing things as they truly are. This idea carries forward into later mystical and occult traditions, where the sun is often associated with divine wisdom, consciousness, and the higher self. It represents the light of awareness that dispels illusion, guiding seekers towards truth and understanding.

In both mythology and spiritual practice, the sun stands as a symbol of revelation. It does not create what is hidden, but it brings it into sight, making the unknown known. Helios's mythological role reminds us that to see clearly—whether in the physical world or in the realm of spirit—is to hold a power both illuminating and inescapable. The light of the sun reveals all, but with that revelation comes responsibility: to acknowledge, to understand, and, ultimately, to act upon what has been seen. When writing about this system in her book *The Witches' Runes*, Heather made similar connections with this stone, to Helios and also to Apollo.[42]

Icarus

The story of Icarus is one of the most enduring cautionary tales in Greek mythology, woven with themes of ambition, hubris, and the harsh justice of natural law. It tells of a young man who, alongside his father, Daedalus, seeks to escape imprisonment by crafting wings of wax and feathers. Before taking flight, Daedalus warns his son to follow a measured path—neither too close to the sea, where the damp air might weigh him down, nor too near the sun, whose heat would melt the wax that binds his wings. Yet, intoxicated by the exhilaration of flight, Icarus soars higher and higher, disregarding his father's wisdom. The sun, in its unrelenting truth, exposes his error, melting the wax and sending him plummeting into the sea.[43]

At its core, this myth is often read as a lesson on hubris—the overreaching pride that leads mortals to their downfall. Icarus's ambition to rise beyond his limits, to touch the realm of the gods, results in his undoing. The sun here plays a dual role: It is both the source of light and revelation, exposing the false strength of Icarus's wings, and the impartial force of justice, delivering consequences without mercy.

Beyond a simple warning against arrogance, Icarus's tale speaks to a deeper tension between human aspiration and natural law. His fatal ascent can be seen as both foolish and noble. He defies the boundaries set before him, reaching for something greater, even at the cost of his life. This duality makes the myth so compelling—while it warns against reckless ambition, it also acknowledges

42. Heather, *The Witches' Runes*.
43. Ovid, *Metamorphoses: Book VIII*, 303–5.

the irresistible pull of transcendence, of seeking beyond what is deemed safe or permissible.

The image of Icarus falling has been revisited time and again in art, literature, and philosophy, each retelling offering a slightly different shade of meaning. To some, it is a story of failure and punishment; to others, it is a tragic but beautiful attempt to reach beyond mortal constraints. Either way, the sun remains central to the story. It is the great revealer, the ultimate judge, and the force that reminds all who seek to rise that truth cannot be escaped. This also resonates with later esoteric traditions, where the sun is not only a giver of life but also a symbol of ultimate truth—one that burns away illusion and reveals the world as it truly is.[44]

Apollo and Duality

The sun can be seen to govern both healing and disease, embodying a powerful duality that reflects its life-giving and destructive aspects. For example, Apollo, a later sun god in Greek mythology, is not only a deity of light, music, and healing but also a bringer of plague and punishment. This dual nature is evident in *The Iliad*, where Apollo sends a devastating plague upon the Greek army after his priest, Chryses, is dishonoured by the king, Agamemnon. In response to the insult, Apollo descends from Olympus, his silver bow gleaming, and unleashes his wrath, raining disease upon the soldiers until they are forced to appease him.[45]

This story illustrates the solar principle in its full scope: Apollo, as a god of healing, can withdraw or withhold health just as easily as he bestows it. His arrows, which strike down the Greeks, mirror the scorching power of the sun, which can bring both growth and drought, nourishment and destruction.[46] In this way, the myths of Apollo—and similar solar deities—highlight how health and illness are interconnected, with balance being the key to harmony.

The Tarot

In the classic Rider-Waite-Smith tarot system, the Sun is the nineteenth card of the major arcana. Cocreator Arthur Edward Waite associated it with the attainment of knowledge and the victory of the conscious mind over unconscious fears,

---

44. Mastronarde, *Preliminary Studies on the Scholia to Euripides*, 149–50.
45. Homer, *The Iliad*, 2–5.
46. Fry, *Troy*, 25–26.

aligning with the Hermetic worldview of the Golden Dawn tradition. He also linked the card to material happiness, fortunate marriage, and contentment. More broadly, it is a positive card, signifying success, wealth, and vitality.[47]

Astrology

In Western astrology, the sun represents the very essence of an individual—their energy, vitality, and core identity. It is the centre of the natal chart, much like it is the centre of the solar system, radiating influence over one's fundamental sense of self. The sun governs willpower, personal expression, and the ego, symbolising the driving force behind a person's life path and sense of purpose. It reflects the qualities that shape one's authentic nature, the traits that remain constant even as circumstances change.

The sun sign, determined by the position of the sun at the moment of an individual's birth, is the most well-known aspect of astrology. When people casually mention their "star sign," they are typically referring to their sun sign, which offers insight into their core motivations, ambitions, and ways of engaging with the world. However, while the sun sign provides a strong foundation for understanding personality, it interacts with other planetary influences in a birth chart, meaning that two people with the same sun sign may express its qualities in very different ways.

Beyond personality, the sun is also associated with vitality and life force, influencing one's overall energy levels and capacity for self-renewal. A well-aspected sun in a birth chart can indicate confidence, purpose, and resilience, while challenges to the sun's placement may manifest as struggles with self-doubt, identity, or direction in life. In this way, the sun serves as both a guiding light and a source of inner strength, illuminating the path towards personal fulfilment and self-realisation.

The Tree of Life

On the Kabbalistic Tree of Life, the sun corresponds to Tiphareth, the Sephirah of Beauty. Positioned as the sixth Sephirah, Tiphareth serves as a harmonising force, connecting to all other Sephiroth except Malkuth. Much like the sun in

47. Waite, *The Pictorial Key to the Tarot*, 144–47.

other systems, Tiphareth is tied to the concept of the self and is associated with spirituality, compassion, and, in some traditions, the Holy Guardian Angel.[48]

The Grimoires

In *Key of Solomon*, a grimoire created in the fourteenth or fifteenth century, the sun is associated with magic related to worldly wealth, hope, games of chance, fortune, divination, and gaining favour with princes. It is also invoked to dissolve hostility and foster friendship. Solar pentacles from the grimoire focus on power, prestige, wealth, freedom, command, and visibility.[49]

In Action

The following activities will help you to engage the energies of the sun through your embodied experience.

Sun Sense Exercise

Encounter the sun at its various points. Get up early to greet the sun as it rises. Observe the shift in light and how the world around you responds to the arriving day. Spend some time with the sun on your skin. Be sure to practice sun safety here and pay attention to your skin to avoid sunburn. This is also an aspect of your personal relationship with the sun. Notice how the warmth feels on your skin and how the quality of the sun changes through the day. Finally, observe the sun as it sets. How does it differ from the rising sun? How does the world respond to this transition?

Take a moment to consider what thoughts and sensations arise within you as you observe these various points of the sun's passage. You can do this over the course of a day or split it up over a few days. If you want to take it a step further, you could practice these observations over the course of a whole year and note the sun's qualities through the changing seasons. Incidentally, this is a wonderful exercise for getting to know your local spirits and the land around you.

---

48. Knight, *A Practical Guide to Qabalistic Symbolism*, 137–49.
49. Solomon, *The Key of Solomon the King*, 97–103.

Sun Energy Exercise

Take yourself outside on a sunny day. Let the sunlight fall on you, and close your eyes. Take a moment to feel the sensations of the light, as in the previous observation exercise. Now, see the light as being full of golden energy. This is the energy of the sun. As you breathe in, see the light entering your body and filling you up. After a few breaths, see this light circulating around your body as you breathe in and out. How does it feel? Can you concentrate it into different parts of your body? When you are done, breathe the energy out and open your eyes. Don't forget to journal any impressions or insights you have with this exercise.

It is worth stating here that energy hygiene traditionally advises that you should ground out any excess energy after an exercise like this. To do this, imagine roots extending from your feet into the earth below (ideally, do this while barefoot outside). Allow any excess energy to flow into the earth, setting the intention to retain the optimum balanced energy for your body.

Make Your Own Sun Stone

Before choosing a stone for the Sun rune, take some time to reflect on the role of the sun in mythology and symbolism, as well as your own experiences with its energy. Work through the exercises in this chapter to deepen your understanding. When you feel ready, begin looking for a stone that resonates with this rune. Keep in mind that your full set should be comfortable to hold during a reading, so avoid anything too large or awkwardly shaped. If you're unsure where to start, you may find it helpful to revisit the "Selecting Your Stones" section from chapter 2. Let your knowledge of the Sun rune guide you as you search, staying open to intuition and signs along the way.

Once you have a stone that feels like a good fit, carry it with you for at least a week. This helps establish a connection and ensures that it truly aligns with the rune's energy. If, after this time, it doesn't feel quite right, return it to its original place with gratitude and continue looking.

You may find it beneficial to hold your chosen stone while working through the remaining exercises in this chapter, though this is entirely optional. If you haven't found the right stone yet, you can still move forward with the exercises while keeping your search in mind. A guided meditation can also be a useful tool for setting your intention and asking for guidance in selecting the right stone.

If you don't yet have a stone, you can temporarily use a hand-drawn version of the rune as a focal point. Treat it with the same level of respect and intention as you would the physical stone. Right now, what matters most is your connection to the rune, not the specific form it takes.

In Thought

As with the previous rune, the first step is to get familiar with the Sun symbol. Study the symbol earlier in this chapter until you can hold it clearly in your mind and visualise it with your eyes closed. The first meditation is unscripted and will focus on allowing the symbol to speak to you through mental impressions, whilst the second will bring you into contact with the spirit of the rune itself.

Meditation 1: Exploring the Sun Stone

The following meditation focuses on building a connection with the image of the rune. The objective is to notice any existing concepts or associations that this rune might hold for you. By performing this exercise, you will be able to witness those ideas bubbling to the surface. Take note of anything that comes up and remember there is no right or wrong here. Spend some time recording anything that comes up in your journal when you are done.

Get into a comfortable position, ensuring your back is straight and supported. Only lie down if you are able to relax without falling asleep. Close your eyes and take several calming breaths. Spend a minute or two here to settle into the exercise and set the intention to explore the symbol of this rune.

Now, with your eyes still closed, see the symbol of the Sun. See it as clearly as you can, holding it in your imagination. You do not have to do anything else; simply regard the symbol and be open to insights. Take note of anything that comes up for you during this time. Are there particular ideas, memories, or sensations that come to you? Take note of these things while letting your attention remain resting gently on the symbol of the Sun.

If you happen to notice that your focus has wandered away to something else, tenderly bring your attention back to the symbol. Try to remain in this meditation for at least ten minutes.

You might like to perform this meditation several times as you work with this rune. You can also revisit it periodically to integrate new insights as your relationship grows.

Meditation 2: Meeting the Spirit of the Sun Rune

As this is a longer meditation, you may want to record the script and listen along as you do the meditation. Otherwise, learn the journey and work through it from memory. You can play soft music, burn some light incense, and set the scene or simply get comfortable and let it happen. For best results, find a space that is private and ensure you won't be disturbed.

Begin by finding a comfortable position and closing your eyes. Take several deep, calming breaths, and let your body relax.

Take a deep breath in… and as you exhale, let go of any tension in your body. Allow yourself to settle into this moment, leaving behind any distractions or concerns. With each breath, feel yourself becoming more relaxed, more at ease.

Now, imagine yourself standing in a beautiful forest. The air is cool and fresh, and the sound of leaves rustling in the gentle breeze surrounds you. Sunlight filters through the canopy above, casting a soft dappled light onto the forest floor.

Take a moment to feel the soil beneath your feet. The earth is solid, grounding you. Each breath you take connects you more deeply with this peaceful place.

As you walk through the forest, you notice a large, ancient tree ahead of you. Its trunk is wide and strong, its bark thick and textured. There's something magical about this tree—it's as though it has been standing here for centuries, watching over the forest.

You feel drawn to the tree. As you get closer, you notice something remarkable: there is a doorway in the trunk of the tree. It's small and rounded, just large enough for you to step through. The door itself is made of smooth wood, with intricate carvings that seem to shimmer slightly in the sunlight.

Take a moment to observe this doorway. What does it look like? Notice the details, the carvings, the way it feels as you gently reach out and touch it.

Now, when you're ready, place your hand on the door's handle. It opens easily, inviting you to step inside. Take a deep breath, and with your next exhale, step through the doorway.

As you pass through, you enter a new space. This place is calm and safe, a sanctuary just for you. Perhaps it's a beautiful garden, a peaceful meadow, or a cosy room—whatever feels right to you. Take a moment to explore this space. Feel the peace that surrounds you. You are safe here, and everything you need is already within you.

Breathe in deeply and let yourself relax even further. In this place, you are free from any worries or stress. Feel the calm washing over you, nurturing and restoring your mind and body.

Take some time here, in this space of peace and tranquillity. You can return to this place anytime you wish, simply by stepping through the doorway in the tree.

As you stand in your sacred space, the place you entered through the doorway, you begin to notice something glowing in the distance. It's a warm, radiant light, growing brighter the more you focus on it. You feel drawn to this light, and as you walk towards it, you see that it forms the shape of a rune—a bright, glowing symbol.

This is the Sun rune. The light it radiates is golden, filling the air with warmth and energy. You can feel its presence like the sun itself, filling your body with life and vitality. Take a moment to stand before the Sun rune. Notice its shape, its brilliance, and the warmth that surrounds you.

The Sun rune represents life, power, illumination, and growth. It is the energy that fuels all living things, the light that guides us through darkness. It offers the power to transform, to shine brightly, and to embrace your fullest potential.

Breathe deeply, allowing the energy of the Sun rune to fill you. Feel the warmth spread through your body, bringing with it a sense of renewal and strength. As you connect with this powerful symbol, you become aware of another presence. It is the spirit of the Sun rune, a guiding force that embodies the energy and wisdom of the sun.

The spirit may appear as a figure of light, a radiant being, or simply a powerful sense of presence. There is no need to force an image. Let the spirit come to you in whatever form feels natural. As the spirit draws closer, you feel its energy—strong, warm, and comforting.

The spirit of the Sun rune greets you with kindness and power. It carries the energy of life, growth, and clarity, and it is here to offer its wisdom to you.

Take a moment to connect with this spirit. Feel the strength of the sun radiating from it, filling you with light and purpose. This spirit is here to help you illuminate your path, to show you where you can grow and shine in your life.

The spirit now invites you to reflect on an area of your life where you wish to bring more light—where you want to grow, to expand, or to let your true self shine more brightly. Take a moment to think about this. Is there a part of your life where you've been hiding your light, holding back from your full potential?

When you are ready, silently or aloud, ask the spirit of the Sun rune for guidance. Ask it to show you how to bring more light and energy into this part of your life.

(Pause for reflection, allowing time to ask and connect.)

The spirit responds, not necessarily with words but with feelings, images, or a deep sense of knowing. It may show you where you need to focus your energy or how to bring more light to a situation or aspect of yourself. Trust in what you receive, even if it is subtle. The Sun rune teaches us to trust the light within us—to allow it to grow and illuminate our path.

Take a moment to sit with this guidance. Know that the sun's energy is always available to you, ready to be called upon whenever you need strength, clarity, or vitality.

Now, the spirit of the Sun rune offers you one final gift—a message, a symbol, or a piece of wisdom that will help you shine even more brightly in your life. Open your heart and mind to receive this final message.

(Pause briefly to receive the message.)

As your time with the spirit of the Sun rune comes to an end, you feel a deep sense of gratitude. The spirit slowly begins to fade, but the warmth and energy of the Sun rune remain, filling the space around you.

Take a deep breath, knowing that you can always return to this place and this spirit whenever you seek guidance or renewal. The light of the sun is always within you, ready to fuel your growth and illuminate your path.

Now, turn away from the rune and begin to walk back towards the doorway in the tree. As you move through your space, you carry the light of the sun within you, knowing that this energy will continue to guide and support you.

Step through the doorway once again, returning to the forest. Feel the warmth of the sun on your skin, hear the soft rustling of the trees in the gentle breeze, and sense the calm of nature around you.

With each breath, bring yourself back to the present moment. Begin to notice your body again, feeling the surface beneath you, the air on your skin.

When you are ready, gently open your eyes, feeling refreshed, empowered, and filled with the light of the Sun rune.

Once you've completed the exercise, take some time to reflect on your experience. What did you observe? What insights did you gain? Did anything unexpected arise? Writing down your thoughts can help solidify your understanding, and if any particularly vivid imagery emerged during your meditation, consider sketching it as a way to anchor it in the physical world.

To fully return to the present moment, you may find a grounding practice helpful. This could be as simple as standing barefoot on the earth and visualising roots extending from your feet into the ground, allowing your energy to stabilise. Alternatively, you might lower your forehead to the floor for a few moments, bringing a sense of connection and balance, before moving on with your day.

In Words

Take the time now to reflect on the experience of connecting with and making your Sun rune. Were there any interpretations and ideas of the sun's symbolism that resonated with you? Why? Do any of the ideas make you uncomfortable or create a sense of resistance? Explore these feelings. What associations do you hold, personally, for the sun?

Research at least one myth about the sun. Write it down and explore its symbolism and messages. How could this inform your interpretation of the Sun stone in a reading? You might like to try writing your own path working to encounter a character from your selected myth and see if you can gain any further wisdom in this way.

Make sure to record your experiences with the exercises, activities, and meditations. Pay attention to any recurring themes that may point to how the sun is presenting in your own imaginal landscape at present.

Chapter Five
The Moon Stone

The Moon stone represents delays, unseen forces (usually hostile) acting on the querent, or a clouding of perspectives because of emotion. It usually depicts a crescent moon—usually as a simple outline not unlike the moon symbol in alchemy. Whether it's waxing or waning is left to the interpretation of the reader and their location on this planet: A waxing crescent moon in the Southern Hemisphere faces in the opposite direction of the waxing crescent moon of our friends in the Northern Hemisphere. Some folks use a darker stone for the Moon stone or draw the symbol in white or silver, as first written about by Crowther in the early 1980s.[50]

In a Reading

With its simple crescent moon image, the Moon stone often speaks of clouded vision, dreams, or things that are not yet known by the querent. It can sometimes counteract the presence of other stones, indicating complications or misunderstandings.

In many respects, the Moon is the counterpart to and opposite of the Sun stone. It is seen as representing feminine energy or influence, as well as delays, detours, and diversion. These can be through clouded perspectives, motions, or oppositional efforts or circumstances obstructing the way. There is an element of being led astray

50. Crowther, *Lid Off the Cauldron*, 110–14.

or misunderstanding what you perceive—both situations that can slow down or impede your progress or growth.

In Culture and Mythology

The moon, like the sun, holds profound significance in mythology and symbolism. Its presence in art and story can be known to represent hidden mysteries, an unclear path, otherworldly beauty, and magic and witchcraft. Its interpretations are vast and varied. Following are a few key connections to help you explore this rich celestial figure.

Selene

In Greek mythology, Selene, the sister of Helios (the sun) and Eos (the dawn), personifies the moon. She rides a horse-drawn chariot across the night sky. Her secondary name, Mene, derives from the Proto-Indo-European moon god and is the root of our modern words *month* and *moon*. In Greek, *Mene* was also linked with measurement, a concept later applied to the moon's role in European occultism.[51]

Selene is mythically associated with Endymion, whom she loved as he lay in eternal sleep. The varying reasons for Endymion's slumber shape the symbolic connection between the moon, sleep, and dreams.

Diana

The Roman goddess of the moon, Diana, is linked to the wilderness, the hunt, and the countryside. As a deity, she bridged the divide between civilisation and the wild. Often depicted in triple form (Diana Triformis), she was associated with other goddesses such as Hecate, Luna (the Roman counterpart of Selene), and Artemis. These associations sometimes reflect the moon's phases or Diana's various roles as huntress, moon goddess, and Underworld figure.

She is also connected with crossroads and transitions, possibly contributing to her association with Hecate. Diana's other domains include childbirth and fame, and she was revered as family patron in Roman household rituals.[52]

---

51. Etymology Online, "Moon," accessed February 2025, https://www.etymonline.com/word/moon.
52. Bulfinch, *Bullfinch's Mythology*, 899.

Thoth

In Egyptian mythology, Thoth, often depicted with an ibis head, governed the moon, knowledge, scribes, art, and magic, and played a role in the judgement of the dead. As the consort of Ma'at (goddess of truth and harmony), Thoth's connection to wisdom was further solidified. He was considered self-created and credited with the invention of science, philosophy, and magic, leading to his later syncretisation with Hermes.

In one myth, Thoth plays a game against the moon god Khonsu, winning enough light to create additional days in the year. This dimmed the moon's light and allowed Nut (the sky) to give birth to other gods, such as Isis and Osiris. This myth underscores the moon's ties to childbirth, wisdom, and the elements of risk and cunning.

The Tarot

In the Rider-Waite-Smith tarot system, the Moon card is the eighteenth trump of the major arcana and is often associated with deception and illusion. It suggests a time when things may not be as they seem, possibly due to misunderstanding, hidden information, or avoidance. Some also link the card to the unconscious mind, reflecting the fear and uncertainty that arise when the conscious mind encounters the unknown.[53] This tension also highlights the dangers of repressing intuition or denying instincts for the sake of comfort.

The Tree of Life

In Kabbalistic teachings, the Sephirah Yesod, meaning "Foundation," is associated with the Moon.[54] Yesod acts as a gateway, connecting the Earth (Malkuth) to the higher realms of the Tree of Life. It balances intellect and emotion, channelling higher energies into the material world. Due to its connection with Malkuth, Yesod is sometimes linked to the sexual organs and is seen as the foundation of physical reality.

53. Waite, *The Pictorial Key to the Tarot*, 140–43.
54. Rankine and d'Este, *Practical Qabalah Magick*, 40–41.

Wicca

In the Wiccan religion, the goddess of the moon is often revered as a symbol of magic, sex, fertility, nature, and the cycle of life, death, and rebirth. She has accumulated many attributes through syncretism with other deities and is commonly worshipped during the full moon. Some regard her as the mother of witches.

The Grimoires

The moon is associated with various spirits and angels in occult literature, notably the Archangel Gabriel. According to the grimoire *Key of Solomon*, lunar magic is favourable for embassies, voyages, messages, navigation, reconciliation, love, and acquiring goods by water. It is also useful for recovering stolen property, obtaining visions, summoning spirits in dreams, and water-related spells.

The Heptameron, a grimoire believed to have been written in the seventeenth century, states that the spirits of the moon "give silver, transport objects, make horses swift, and reveal secrets of the present and future."[55]

In Action

The following exercises will help you to gain an embodied experience of the moon's energy both from an observational and an energetic level.

Moon Observation

Take time to bask in the moonlight, gazing upon the moon. Check in with your senses and note how you feel as you share this time with the moon. What is the quality of the night around you, and how does the moon impact this feeling? What animals are present? What activities are taking place around you? You might like to try this exercise each night for a full lunar cycle to get a feel for the nuance of its phases.

Moon Energy

Go outside on a clear night when the moon is visible. Let its light fall on you and close your eyes. Take a moment to feel the sensations of the light, as in the observation exercise. Now, see the light as being full of silver energy. This is the energy of the moon. As you breathe in, see the light entering your body and filling you up.

---

55. Turner, *Henry Cornelius Agrippa's Fourth Book of Occult Philosophy*, 92.

After a few breaths, see this light circulating around your body as you breathe in and out. How does it feel? Can you concentrate it into different parts of your body?

As with the energy exercise for the Sun rune, be sure to finish this practice by grounding out any excess energy.

Make Your Own Moon Stone

Before creating your Moon rune stone, take some time to explore the moon's symbolism and how it has been understood across different myths and traditions. As we have explored earlier in this chapter, the moon is often associated with intuition, cycles of change, hidden knowledge, and deep emotional currents. Consider your own experiences with lunar energy—how do you feel under a full moon or a dark moon? How do its cycles influence your emotions, creativity, or dreams? Working through the exercises in this chapter will help you develop a clearer sense of the moon's significance and how it connects to this rune.

When you feel ready, begin searching for a stone that suits the Moon rune. Let your intuition guide you, paying attention to a stone's texture, colour, weight, and the feeling it evokes. Does it remind you of moonlight, reflection, or the quiet pull of unseen forces? Keep in mind that your full rune set should be comfortable to hold and use in a reading, so choose a stone that fits well in your hands. If you're unsure where to start, you may find it helpful to revisit the guidance on selecting stones in chapter 2.

Once you have chosen a stone, carry it with you for at least a week to build a connection. Notice any changes in your awareness, any dreams or insights that arise while keeping it close. If, after this time, the stone doesn't feel quite right, return it respectfully to where you found it and continue your search.

When you are ready to mark your rune, use the method that feels most natural to you, whether it is painting, engraving, or another technique. Approach this process with focus and intention, allowing yourself to connect with the deeper meaning of the Moon rune as you work. You may also wish to hold your stone while completing the remaining exercises in this chapter, though this is optional.

If you have not yet found the right stone, try using a hand-drawn version of the rune as a temporary focal point, treating it with the same level of intention and respect as you would a physical stone. What matters most is your relationship with the rune and what it represents, not the specific form that it takes. You can always return to these exercises to build the connection with a stone when you find it.

In Thought

Take some time to get familiar with the Moon symbol earlier in this chapter. It will be important to be able to see it clearly in your mind for the exercises in this section. Study the symbol until you can visualise it with your eyes closed and then proceed. As in the previous two chapters, the first meditation will focus on allowing the symbol to speak to you, and the second meditation is a guided meditation.

Meditation 1: Exploring the Moon Stone

The following meditation is unscripted and will allow you to build a connection with the image of the rune. The objective is to notice any existing concepts or associations that this rune might hold for you. By performing this exercise, you will be able to witness those ideas bubbling to the surface. Take note of anything that comes up and remember there is no right or wrong here. Spend some time recording anything that comes up in your journal when you are done.

Find a comfortable position but avoid lying down unless you can remain relaxed without falling asleep. Ensure your back is straight and supported. Close your eyes and take several deep, calming breaths. Take a moment to check in with your body, releasing any tension. Allow your breath to dissolve and carry away any stress as your body softens and relaxes. Spend a minute or two here to settle into the practice, setting your intention to explore the symbol of this rune.

With your eyes still closed, envision the symbol of the Moon. Hold it clearly in your imagination without any effort, simply observing it and being open to any insights that arise. Pay attention to any thoughts, ideas, or memories that surface. Do particular themes emerge? Are there sensations in your body? Note these observations while gently keeping your focus on the Moon symbol.

If you find your attention wandering, gently guide it back to the symbol. Aim to stay in this meditation for at least ten minutes.

You may also choose to repeat this meditation as you work with the rune, returning to it over time to deepen your insights and connection.

Meditation 2: Meeting the Spirit of the Moon Rune

As this is a longer meditation, you may want to record the script and listen along as you do the meditation. Otherwise, learn the journey and work through it from memory. You can play soft music, burn some light incense, and set the scene or simply get comfortable and let it happen. For best results, find a space that is private and ensure you won't be disturbed.

Begin by finding a comfortable position and closing your eyes. Take several deep, calming breaths, and let your body relax.

Take a deep breath in… and as you exhale, let go of any tension in your body. Allow yourself to settle into this moment, leaving behind any distractions or concerns. With each breath, feel yourself becoming more relaxed, more at ease.

Now, imagine yourself standing in a beautiful forest. The air is cool and fresh, and the sound of leaves rustling in the gentle breeze surrounds you. Moonlight filters through the canopy above, casting a soft, dappled light onto the forest floor.

Take a moment to feel the soil beneath your feet. The earth is solid, grounding you. Each breath you take connects you more deeply with this peaceful place.

As you walk through the forest, you notice a large, ancient tree ahead of you. Its trunk is wide and strong, its bark thick and textured. There's something magical about this tree—it's as though it has been standing here for centuries, watching over the forest.

You feel drawn to the tree. As you get closer, you notice something remarkable: There is a doorway in the trunk of the tree. It's small and rounded, just large enough for you to step through. The door itself is made of smooth wood, with intricate carvings that seem to shimmer slightly in the sunlight.

Take a moment to observe this doorway. What does it look like? Notice the details, the carvings, the way it feels as you gently reach out and touch it.

Now, when you're ready, place your hand on the door's handle. It opens easily, inviting you to step inside. Take a deep breath, and with your next exhale, step through the doorway.

As you pass through, you enter a new space. This place is calm and safe, a sanctuary just for you. Perhaps it's a beautiful garden, a peaceful meadow, or a cosy room—whatever feels right to you. Take a moment to explore this space. Feel the peace that surrounds you. You are safe here, and everything you need is already within you.

Breathe in deeply and let yourself relax even further. In this place, you are free from any worries or stress. Feel the calm washing over you, nurturing and restoring your mind and body.

Take some time here, in this space of peace and tranquillity. You can return to this place anytime you wish, simply by stepping through the doorway in the tree.

As you find yourself in your peaceful space, you are enveloped in a sense of calm. The light in this place softens, and as you look around, you notice a gentle glow emerging in the distance. It is a cool, silvery light, peaceful and inviting. As you walk towards it, you begin to see the outline of a rune taking shape—a symbol glowing softly in the darkness.

This is the Moon rune. Its presence feels quiet and mysterious yet deeply comforting. The light of the Moon rune is gentle but constant, illuminating the space around you with its soft glow. Take a moment to observe this rune. Notice its shape, the way it glows in the dim light, and the way it makes you feel.

The Moon rune represents intuition, mystery, cycles, and the hidden aspects of the self. It is the light that guides us through the darkness, helping us trust our inner wisdom when the path ahead isn't fully clear. As you stand before the Moon rune, you feel its calm energy wrapping around you like a blanket of stillness and serenity.

Breathe deeply, allowing the energy of the Moon rune to fill you. Feel its calming light enter your body, quieting your mind and tuning you into your inner self. As you connect with the energy of the Moon rune, you become aware of a presence nearby—a spirit connected to this rune, a guide that embodies the wisdom of the moon.

This is the spirit of the Moon rune, a being of quiet power and deep intuition. It may take the form of a figure cloaked in silver light, a soft glowing presence, or a shadowy figure that is both mysterious and comforting. There is no need to force an image—allow the spirit to appear in whatever form feels natural to you.

As the spirit approaches, you feel its calmness, its connection to the deeper mysteries of life. It carries the wisdom of the moon—of the cycles of life, the unseen forces at work, and the power of intuition. The spirit greets you with gentle energy, inviting you to explore the hidden aspects of yourself.

Take a moment to connect with this spirit. Feel its deep calm, its knowledge of things unseen and unknown. The spirit of the Moon rune is here to help you see beyond the surface and understand the deeper truths within yourself and the world around you.

The spirit now invites you to reflect on an aspect of your life where you seek greater clarity or understanding—an area that feels uncertain or unknown. Perhaps there is something hidden that you wish to bring to light. Or maybe there is a part of yourself that you want to explore more deeply. When you are ready, silently or aloud, ask the spirit of the Moon rune for guidance. Ask it to help you see what is hidden, to trust your intuition, and to understand the cycles of your life.

(Pause for reflection, allowing time to ask and connect.)

The spirit may not speak in direct words but through feelings, images, or symbols. It may show you something subtle yet meaningful, helping you to understand the ebb and flow of your life or guiding you to trust your inner knowing. Allow yourself to receive this wisdom, even if it feels abstract or elusive. The Moon rune teaches us to trust the deeper rhythms and cycles that guide us, even when we cannot see the full picture.

Take a moment to sit with this wisdom. Feel how the energy of the moon gently illuminates what has been hidden, helping you to see with new eyes. Know that whatever guidance you've received is for your highest good and that the moon's light is always available to guide you, even in the darkest moments.

Now, the spirit of the Moon rune offers you a final message—a gift of insight or wisdom that you can carry with you as you move forward in your life. Open your heart and mind to receive this final message.

(Pause briefly to receive the message.)

As your time with the spirit of the Moon rune comes to an end, you feel a deep sense of peace and gratitude. The spirit slowly begins to fade, but the soft glow of the Moon rune remains, filling the space with calm and clarity.

Take a deep breath, knowing that you can return to this space and this spirit whenever you seek guidance or comfort. The light of the moon is always within you, quietly guiding you through the cycles of life.

Now, turn away from the Moon rune and begin to walk back toward the doorway in the tree. As you move through this peaceful space, you carry the moon's calm energy within you, knowing that its light will continue to illuminate your path, even when things are unclear.

Step through the doorway once more, returning to the forest. Feel the soft light of the moon above you, casting a gentle glow through the trees. Hear the rustling of the leaves in the breeze and sense the quiet calm of the forest around you.

With each breath, bring yourself back to the present moment. Begin to notice your body again, feeling the surface beneath you, the air on your skin.

When you are ready, gently open your eyes, feeling calm, centred, and connected to the deep wisdom of the Moon rune.

When you have finished, take a moment to record your insights: What did you see? What have you learnt? Did anything surprise you? As part of your records, you can sketch out any particularly vivid imagery that came through your meditation as a way of grounding it into the physical world.

You might also like to try a grounding exercise to help bring you back to the present moment. This can be achieved by standing barefoot on the earth, imagining energetic roots reaching from your feet into the ground and balancing your energy, or resting your forehead on the floor for a moment.

In Words

Consider what you already know about the moon. How has it been described in myths, stories, and scientific understanding? To deepen your knowledge, take a trip to the library or explore reputable sources to research its significance.

Start by looking into the moon's relationship with the tides and the earth. The gravitational pull between the moon and our planet plays a crucial role in the movement of the oceans, creating the rhythmic rise and fall of tides. This celestial dance has long been woven into folklore, often linking the moon's cycles to themes of change, balance, and hidden forces at work.

Next, explore the science behind the moon's phases. Why does it appear to change shape in the sky? How do its waxing and waning cycles occur? Understanding the mechanics of lunar phases—how the moon reflects sunlight and moves in relation to the Earth and sun—can provide insight into why different cultures have attributed various meanings to each stage of its cycle.

As you gather these details, consider how they connect to the stories we tell about the moon and its power. Many traditions link the moon to intuition, transformation, and cycles of renewal. How might the physical realities of the moon's motion have shaped these beliefs? By combining scientific knowledge with symbolic meaning, you can develop a richer understanding of how the moon's influence is perceived in both practical and mystical terms.

Be sure to journal your notes from the meditation exercises along with any interesting information from your personal research.

Chapter Six
The Rings Stone

The Rings stone often represents marriage or joining. It signifies bonds of commitment, whether in relationships, partnerships, or agreements, and reflects the interplay between individuals, ideas, or energies coming together in harmony or obligation. It usually displays three overlapping rings, but interestingly, Ashcroft-Nowicki's original article depicts them as being separate from one another. In the versions of the Witches' Runes written about by Sheppard, this stone is known as Romance and bears the image of a triquetra,[56] a three-petaled glyph that often appears in Celtic knotwork. West (and, earlier, Crowther) stipulated this symbol should be painted in pink,[57] but this is not common in sets that we have seen or worked with.

In a Reading

The symbol typically consists of three interlocking circles, though sometimes only two are used. It represents the bond between two entities and their connection, while also symbolising the creation of something new through their union. The overlap between the two independent rings signifies the formation of something greater than the sum of its parts.

While marriage and relationships are common interpretations, they are just examples of the symbol's broader meaning. It can also represent partnerships in

56. Sheppard, *A Witch's Runes*, 55.
57. West, *The Real Witches' Book of Spells and Rituals.*

business, collaborative projects, or commitments to a goal or ideal. At its core, the Rings rune expresses the concept of two things intertwining or joining together.

In Culture and Mythology

Rings, especially magic rings, are a common motif in myth, story, and folklore. These stories often focus on the magical or transformative acts undertaken to forge the rings, or on the powers these rings bestow on their wearers.

The Ring Cycle

This is a collection of four operas composed by Richard Wagner in 1857, each rooted in Germanic mythology and centred around a ring of power. The ring is forged from gold taken from the Rhine River, a source of immense power. However, the ring's power comes at a great cost: The one who wields the ring must renounce love. In the first opera, *Das Rheingold,* the ring is created by a man willing to pay this price after being scorned. Naturally, such a powerful object becomes highly coveted, leading to an epic drama that spans some fifteen hours of music.

Today, most people are more familiar with *The Lord of the Rings,* which draws from similar mythological sources. Written by J. R. R. Tolkien and first published in 1954, the famous story effectively captures the binding nature of the ring as a symbol. We see individuals bound to Sauron through their rings, while the One Ring also ties Sauron to Middle-earth. This binding force mirrors the symbolism of placing a ring on someone's finger, though, hopefully, without the dark magic.

Plato's Ring

In *The Republic,* Plato recounts a story of a magic ring with the ability to give its wearer the power of invisibility. The ring is found in a cave and brings out a dark ambition in its finder. The ring's power is used to seduce a queen and murder a king. This speaks to the corrupting quality and moral implications of power.

The Golden Bough

James George Frazer's classic work *The Golden Bough* was a popular source for the early neo-Pagan movement. In this text, he mentions the belief that rings could bind the soul to the body and prevent foreign spirits from entering. In this sense, it functions as a sort of lock. While the protective aspects of this idea are noteworthy, Frazer points out that a ring might provide immortality to its wearer by literally binding the body and soul together. Despite its widespread literary influence, the work has received criticism in the field of anthropology for its outdated approaches to cross-cultural comparison as well as for Frazer's modifying of evidence to support the story he wished to tell.[58]

The Grimoires

Prominently featured in several Solomonic grimoires from the medieval period, particularly the *Ars Goetia* (1600s), the Ring of Solomon is typically regarded with granting the wearer the power to command demons. In the *Lesser Key of Solomon*, it is mentioned for its ability to protect the magician from the harmful fumes emitted by especially dangerous demons.[59]

In the *Testament of Solomon*, the ring is said to have been given to King Solomon by the Archangel Michael in response to his prayers for aid against demons tormenting a man.[60] While variations of this story have evolved over time and across cultures, the central theme remains consistent: The ring symbolises a connection between spirits and humans. It acts as a bridge between worlds, serving as a form of protection and a passport for safe communication—though some tales suggest that this safety is not always guaranteed.

Fairy Rings

While not a piece of wearable jewellery, toadstool circles are rich with myth in European folklore. These natural formations are believed to be places where fairies have danced, or portals to the fairy realm. In British fairy tales, such as "Tam Lin," they often feature in stories of fairy weddings and employment contracts at otherworldly celebrations that last for centuries. These tales explore themes of bonds, their legitimacy and dissolution, and the agency of the individual. Above all, they touch upon ideas of destiny and the enduring—or illusory—nature of true love. Ultimately, they prompt the question: What is the greater bond?

This power of rings to act as gateways and forge contracts finds a reflection in the magical circles used throughout grimoires and Western ritual traditions.

58. Lienhardt, "Frazer's Anthropology."
59. Peterson, *The Lesser Key of Solomon*, 44–45.
60. Solomon, *The Testament of Solomon*, 22.

Borromean Rings

The overlapping rings pattern has appeared in artwork and architecture for centuries and is often used in this way to symbolise strength in unity. When depicted in 3D space, this motif is known as Borromean rings, named for the House of Borromeo, which used the image in its coat of arms from the early Renaissance. To get a clear idea of this image, think of a Venn diagram where each curve weaves in and out of the others to form an over-under pattern.

Borromean rings would come apart if one was removed—one can't exist without the other two. In many branches of Christianity, these rings are used to visually represent the belief in God as one being made up of three distinct beings who exist in equal, eternal communion as Father, Son, and Holy Spirit.[61]

In Action

The Rings rune speaks to the connections we form—whether through love, duty, or shared purpose—and the strength or challenges that arise from these bonds. To truly understand its essence, we must engage with the ways unions shape our lives, from the tangible commitments we make to the unseen ties that influence us. The following exercises will guide you in exploring the symbolism of the Rings rune through reflection, movement, and interaction, helping you to experience its meaning firsthand.

Wear a Ring

Select a ring, whether purchased, handmade, or inherited, wear it each day, and take note of how it subtly influences your mood, thoughts, or sense of self. Does the ring help you feel more grounded or connected? Does it heighten awareness of how you wish to connect with others? Keep a journal of your reactions, from the initial excitement or discomfort to the gradual feelings of connection or symbolism it builds in your life.

Enchant a Ring

Select a ring and dedicate it to a specific intention, such as protection, self-love, or attracting harmony. Perform a ritual or visualisation to imbue the ring with this

61. Cromwell et al.,"The Borromean rings," 53–62.

purpose, and then wear it as often as possible. Observe how the ring influences your energy and mood or how others respond to you while you wear it. Reflect on the experience of carrying a tangible piece of magic and journal any subtle shifts in how you connect with your environment and others.

Create an Artwork or Mandala Using Circles

Gather art supplies and create a piece of artwork out of circles. As you work, consider the symbolism of unity, wholeness, and protection inherent in circular shapes. Arrange the circle to create a sense of flow, interconnection, or containment. Notice what each shape's position suggests: Some may represent boundaries, while others may evoke openness or balance. Reflect on the feeling of completion within the circle and how it relates to the energy of the Ring rune's unifying influence.

Create a Magical Circle

Find a quiet place where you can create a physical circle on the ground with chalk, stones, or any symbolic markers. Step inside and feel the subtle shifts as you enter the enclosed space. Notice any sense of security, boundary, or sacredness that arises. Contemplate the difference between the space within and the world outside, exploring how this affects your thoughts, mood, or awareness. Does this space feel different to the open world beyond? What can this sense of enclosure teach us about the nature of connection?

Create a Circle Alternate: Group

This one cannot be done alone. Find one or two friends who will perform this exercise with you. Stand in a small circle and hold hands, focusing on creating a flow of energy between you. Slowly push and pull energy around the circle, experimenting with sending it clockwise and counterclockwise. Notice how each person's energy changes the flow, creating a shared field of unity and synergy. Reflect on the unique dynamic that emerges, something that no single person could achieve alone, and observe how this act of unity enhances the connection and collective energy of your group. You might like to compare your observations.

Make Your Own Rings Stone

Before crafting your Rings rune stone, take some time to reflect on what this symbol means to you. The Rings rune embodies connection, cycles, unity, and the bonds that shape our lives. Think about the relationships, commitments, and shared paths that have influenced you. You might wish to revisit earlier exercises in this chapter to deepen your understanding before selecting your stone.

When choosing a stone for this rune, look for one that resonates with its themes. You may feel drawn to a naturally smooth or rounded stone, reflecting the idea of continuity, or one with unique markings that suggest interwoven shapes. Let your intuition guide you, but remember that your full set of runes should be comfortable to use, so avoid anything too large or unwieldy. If you need guidance, refer to the "Selecting Your Stones" section in chapter 2 for help.

Once you have chosen a stone, carry it with you for at least a week to build a connection. Pay attention to how it feels in your hand and whether it aligns with the ideas of union and interconnection. If, after this time, the stone doesn't seem right, return it to its original place with gratitude and continue searching.

When you're ready to mark the rune, use your preferred method, whether it's painting, engraving, or another technique. Treat this as an intentional process, focussing on the meaning of the Rings rune as you work. You might reflect on the ties that bind people together, the unseen forces shaping your life, or the cyclical nature of time.

Once completed, your Rings rune stone can serve as a tool for meditation, a point of focus in your practice, or part of your divination work. As you progress through the exercises in this chapter, keep it nearby to strengthen your connection to the rune's themes of unity, reciprocity, and the interwoven nature of existence.

In Thought

Once you have connected with the rings through the myths and exercises, it is time to get to know this symbol better internally. Begin by closely studying the rune symbol until you can clearly visualise it. When you can see it clearly with your eyes closed, you are ready to move on to the meditations. The first meditation exercise is unscripted and can be done with little preparation; however, you might like to record yourself reading the script for the second meditation so that you can be guided through it.

Meditation 1: Exploring the Rings Stones

This first meditation focuses on building a connection with the image of the rune. The objective is to notice any existing concepts or associations that this rune might hold for you. By performing this exercise, you will be able to witness those ideas bubbling to the surface. Take note of anything that comes up and remember there is no right or wrong here. Spend some time recording anything that comes up in your journal when you are done.

Find a comfortable position but avoid lying down unless you can remain relaxed without falling asleep. Ensure your back is straight and supported.

Close your eyes and take several deep, calming breaths. Take a moment to check in with your body, releasing any tension. Allow your breath to dissolve and carry away any stress as your body softens and relaxes. Spend a minute or two here to settle into the practice, setting your intention to explore the symbol of this rune.

Study the Rings symbol until you can hold it in your mind's eye. Enter a meditative state and see the Rings symbol clearly. Do not force, push, or control anything. Remain relaxed and simply watch the symbol. Hold this gentle contemplation for at least ten minutes. Take note of anything that comes up during this time. If you find your attention wandering, gently guide it back to the symbol. Aim to stay in this meditation for at least ten minutes.

You may also choose to repeat this meditation as you work with the rune, returning to it over time to deepen your insights and connection.

Meditation 2: Meeting the Spirit of the Rings Rune

As we noted, you may want to record the following script and listen along as you do this guided meditation. Otherwise, learn the journey and work through it from memory. You can play soft music, burn some light incense and set the scene or simply get comfortable and let it happen. For best results, find a space that is private and ensure you won't be disturbed.

Begin by finding a comfortable position and closing your eyes. Take several deep, calming breaths, and let your body relax.

Take a deep breath in... and as you exhale, let go of any tension in your body. Allow yourself to settle into this moment, leaving behind any distractions or concerns. With each breath, feel yourself becoming more relaxed, more at ease.

Now, imagine yourself standing in a beautiful forest. The air is cool and fresh, and the sound of leaves rustling in the gentle breeze surrounds you. Sunlight filters through the canopy above, casting a soft dappled light onto the forest floor.

Take a moment to feel the soil beneath your feet. The earth is solid, grounding you. Each breath you take connects you more deeply with this peaceful place.

As you walk through the forest, you notice a large, ancient tree ahead of you. Its trunk is wide and strong, its bark thick and textured. There's something magical about this tree—it's as though it has been standing here for centuries, watching over the forest.

You feel drawn to the tree. As you get closer, you notice something remarkable: There is a doorway in the trunk of the tree. It's small and rounded, just large enough for you to step through. The door itself is made of smooth wood, with intricate carvings that seem to shimmer slightly in the sunlight.

Take a moment to observe this doorway. What does it look like? Notice the details, the carvings, the way it feels as you gently reach out and touch it.

Now, when you're ready, place your hand on the door's handle. It opens easily, inviting you to step inside. Take a deep breath, and with your next exhale, step through the doorway.

As you pass through, you enter a new space. This place is calm and safe, a sanctuary just for you. Perhaps it's a beautiful garden, a peaceful meadow, or a cosy room—whatever feels right to you. Take a moment to explore this space. Feel the peace that surrounds you. You are safe here, and everything you need is already within you.

Breathe in deeply and let yourself relax even further. In this place, you are free from any worries or stress. Feel the calm washing over you, nurturing and restoring your mind and body.

Take some time here, in this space of peace and tranquillity. You can return to this place anytime you wish, simply by stepping through the doorway in the tree.

As you stand in your peaceful space, you notice a shift in the air around you. There's a new presence, a gentle energy that seems to pull you forward. As you walk through this space, you notice two golden rings intertwined, glowing softly in the distance. The rings seem to shimmer with warmth and harmony, and as you approach, you realise that this is the Rings rune—a symbol of union, connection, and harmony.

Take a moment to stand before the Rings rune. Notice the way the two rings join, seamlessly connected yet each maintaining its own shape and identity. Feel the energy of this rune as it radiates a sense of togetherness, balance, and wholeness.

The Rings rune represents the power of joining—whether that's the union of two people, the merging of energies, or the integration of different aspects of yourself. It speaks of partnership, connection, and the resultant beauty when things come together in harmony.

Breathe deeply, allowing the energy of the Rings rune to flow into you. Feel it moving through your body, filling you with a sense of unity, balance, and wholeness. As you connect with this rune, you become aware of another presence nearby. This is the spirit of the Rings rune, a guide connected to this symbol, here to offer you wisdom and insight about connection, union, and harmony.

The spirit may appear in the form of a figure intertwined with light, a gentle presence, or an energy that feels whole and complete. There is no need to force an image—allow the spirit to come to you in whatever form feels natural.

As the spirit approaches, you feel a sense of calm and harmony. This being embodies the energy of union—the joining of forces, whether in love, partnership, or the integration of the self. The spirit of the Rings rune greets you warmly, offering its guidance and support.

Take a moment to connect with this spirit. Feel the sense of completeness it carries—the deep understanding that all things are connected and that the power of joining creates something greater than the sum of its parts.

The spirit now invites you to reflect on an aspect of your life where you are seeking connection or harmony. Perhaps you are thinking about a relationship, a partnership, or even the way different aspects of yourself come together. Take a moment to reflect on where you might need balance or integration in your life. When you are ready, silently or aloud, ask the spirit of the Rings rune for guidance. Ask it to help you understand how to create tranquility in this area.

(Pause for reflection, allowing time to ask and connect.)

The spirit may respond with feelings, images, or a sense of knowing. Trust what you receive, even if it feels subtle or abstract. The Rings rune teaches us that connection and harmony come from understanding and integrating the different parts of our lives—whether through relationships with others or through finding balance within ourselves.

Take a moment to sit with this wisdom. Feel how the energy of the Rings rune brings a sense of wholeness and peace, helping you to see the beauty in union and joining. Know that whatever guidance you have received is for your highest good and that the energy of the Rings rune is always available to you whenever you seek balance or connection.

Now, the spirit offers you a final gift—a message or symbol of union and harmony that you can carry with you as you move forward. Open your heart and mind to receive this final message.

(Pause briefly to receive the message.)

As your time with the spirit of the Rings rune comes to an end, you feel a deep sense of peace and gratitude. The spirit slowly begins to fade, but the glowing symbol of the intertwined rings remains, filling the space with warmth and unity.

Take a deep breath, knowing that you can return to this space and this spirit whenever you seek guidance on union or balance. The energy of the Rings rune is always within you, helping you create harmony in your relationships and in yourself.

Now, turn away from the rune and begin to walk back toward the doorway in the tree. As you move through your peaceful space, you carry the feeling of connection and balance within you, knowing that this energy will continue to guide and support you. Step through the doorway once more, returning to the forest. Feel the ground beneath your feet, hear the soft sounds of the leaves in the breeze, and sense the calmness of the forest around you.

With each breath, bring yourself back to the present moment. Begin to notice your body again, feeling the surface beneath you, the air on your skin.

When you are ready, gently open your eyes, feeling calm, connected, and filled with the harmony of the Rings rune.

When you have finished, take a moment to record your insights: What did you see? What have you learnt? Did anything surprise you? As part of your records, you can sketch out any particularly vivid imagery that came through your meditation as a way of grounding it into the physical world.

You might also like to try a grounding exercise to help bring you back to the present moment. This can be achieved by standing barefoot on the earth, imagining energetic roots reaching from your feet into the ground and balancing your energy, or resting your forehead on the floor for a moment.

In Words

Take time to reflect on the symbolism of the Rings rune, considering both the stories you have explored and your own experiences. Use the following prompts as a guide, journaling your thoughts to deepen and consolidate your understanding of this rune.

Begin by examining the commitments in your life. What are you bound to, whether by choice, circumstance, or necessity? These bonds may take many forms—relationships, responsibilities, beliefs, or personal goals. How do these commitments shape your experiences, emotions, and sense of self? Are there lessons they have taught you or challenges they have introduced?

Next, consider the jewellery you wear, if any. Do you wear rings or other adornments regularly? If so, what significance do they hold for you? Are they sentimental, symbolic, or purely decorative? If you do not wear jewellery, is this a conscious choice? Does it reflect something about your values or sense of self? Pay attention to how jewellery, particularly rings, affects the way you feel in your body—does it bring a sense of identity, belonging, or empowerment?

As you move through the meditations, exercises, and journaling prompts, take note of your experiences. What insights emerge as you actively engage with the symbolism of the Rings rune?

Finally, reflect on the role of rings in vows and binding agreements, particularly in marriage. Rings have long been used to seal commitments, carrying both legal and spiritual weight. In this light, do you see rings as magical objects—spells in physical form, seals of intent, or talismans that reinforce a promise? Consider how this perspective influences your understanding of the Rings rune and the power inherent in the bonds we create.

Chapter Seven
The Birds Stone

The Birds stone represents inspiration and the coming of fresh ideas or news. The symbol displays several birds in flight, usually as simple *m*-shaped sketches. Sometimes these will be differing sizes—to indicate distance—but often they are fairly uniform. The Birds stone depicted in Ashcroft-Nowicki's original article shows three birds of roughly even size and the same colour, positioned one above the other. Later iterations of the Witches' Runes, such as those outlined by Nock in 2022, have become more stylised and curled. Nock refers to these shapes as wyverns—mythical, two-legged, winged, dragon-like creatures—in flight, rather than birds.[62]

The Birds stone is the rune of communications, news, and inspiration. With the three birds in flight, this stone can indicate an arrival, a revelation, or even just an information overload.

In a Reading

In a reading, this stone signals the arrival of news or ideas. It represents inspiration, both in the everyday sense and the more ancient notion of channelling the Divine. Depending on its context and proximity to other stones, it can indicate forthcoming revelations, the anticipation of something arriving, or the experience of being overwhelmed by information without discerning its relevance or

62. Nock, *The Modern Witchcraft Guide to Runes*, 16.

importance. Sometimes when it appears next to other stones, it can bring movement to a previously stagnant or stuck situation.

In Culture and Mythology

Birds have long captivated human attention and imagination, featuring prominently in myths, symbolism, art, and even practical roles—from delivering messages through augury to serving as literal post carriers. Their swift flight has solidified their status as beings of the air and messengers between the worlds. The ability to traverse great distances, unhindered by the terrain below, has lent them a mystical aura. As creatures of the air, birds are often seen as bridging realms, and their wings have become symbols of divine messengers and swift-moving entities such as Hermes and angels.

Birds As Messengers

With their powers of flight and agility, birds have long been associated with messages and the spreading of news. Whether in their literal role as postal carriers or in the symbolic wings of angels (from the Greek *angelos*, meaning "messenger"), birds are closely linked to travel, motion, and communication.[63] Their swift, graceful movement through the air reflects the transmission of news, while their varied and intricate songs reinforce their connection to speech and the exchange of ideas.

Owls

Owls have long been creatures of the night across various cultures, symbolising both the unknown and the ability to see into the night—whether the night represents knowledge, death, or spiritual insight. Their mystical presence has made them figures of fascination, embodying complex dualities such as wisdom and fear, life and death, and protection and danger.

In ancient Greece, the owl is most famously linked to Athena, the goddess of wisdom and warfare. Often shown as her companion, the owl became a symbol of knowledge, intelligence, and strategic warfare. However, the Romans viewed

63. Etymology Online, "Angel," accessed February 2025, https://www.etymonline.com/word/angel.

owls in a more foreboding light, believing them to be harbingers of death and misfortune. The screech of an owl was thought to foretell doom, illness, or death.

Huginn and Muninn

In Norse mythology, Huginn and Muninn are a pair of ravens belonging to Odin, the All-Father and chief of the Aesir. These ravens play a crucial role in helping Odin maintain his wisdom and knowledge across the Nine Realms. Their names are deeply symbolic: Huginn means "thought," and Muninn means "memory" or "mind." Together, they embody Odin's omniscience and his connection to both intellectual and spiritual insight.

Huginn and Muninn represent the balance between active thought and passive memory, intellect and intuition. They enable Odin to perceive both the immediate and the eternal, serving as his eyes and ears across the cosmos. Essentially, they are extensions of his mind and consciousness, allowing him to remain aware of what happens in all corners of the world. Their symbolism reflects Norse themes of wisdom, foresight, and the interplay between thought and memory, highlighting the importance of knowledge in Viking society.

Ravens, in general, are powerful symbols in Norse mythology, associated with war, death, and prophecy. They were often seen on the battlefield, feeding on the fallen, and their presence on shields, banners, and other items further emphasised their role as divine emissaries of Odin.[64]

Omens and Augury

Birds have been the bringers of omens or the harbingers of death, shaping cultural beliefs and superstitions for centuries. These varied interpretations reflect the deep connections between human societies and the natural world, with birds often embodying themes of life, death, and transformation.

In ancient Rome, the practice of augury involved interpreting bird behaviour to predict the future. Augurs, priests who performed this ritual, would study the flight patterns, calls, or feeding habits of birds to discern the will of the gods. For example, the direction in which a bird flew—whether to the left or right—was crucial in determining the success or failure of a venture.

---

64. Lafayllve, *A Practical Heathen's Guide to Asatru*, 30.

Magical Birds of Rhiannon

In the stories of Rhiannon from *The Mabinogion*, magical birds are closely tied to her mysterious and otherworldly nature. A figure often associated with the Welsh Otherworld, Rhiannon is a goddess of horses and sovereignty. She is married to Pwyll, a human king, and later becomes the mother of Pryderi. In her story, three magical birds are said to sing so sweetly that they can wake the dead and lull the living to sleep. These birds are associated with the distant Isle of Annwn, the Welsh Otherworld, and are occasionally called the Birds of Rhiannon, though they are not always directly linked to her in the tale.

The birds symbolise the Otherworld's enchanting and transformative power, bridging the mortal world and realms of magic and mystery. Their song represents healing, divine beauty, and transcendence, capable of overcoming pain, grief, and death itself. In the tales, they appear at moments that remind listeners of the Otherworld's omnipresent influence, underscoring themes of longing and the cyclical nature of life and death.

The significance of these birds extends to the Welsh concept of *awen*, or divine inspiration, which carried both sorrow and beauty. Their song exemplifies the powerful connection between sorrow and solace, reminding listeners of the hidden beauty and mystery that lie beyond human perception. Through these magical birds, Rhiannon embodies the divine forces of rebirth and renewal, emphasising her role as both a nurturing mother and a powerful, enigmatic Otherworld figure.[65]

Branwen's Starling

In the tale of Branwen, daughter of Llŷr, from *The Mabinogion*, Branwen is a Welsh princess married to Matholwch, the king of Ireland. The marriage is intended to forge peace between the nations, but it quickly falls apart when her half-brother, Efnysien, insults the Irish by mutilating their horses. Matholwch responds by mistreating Branwen, and she endures years of cruelty and isolation in Ireland. Desperate, Branwen raises a starling and teaches it to carry a message to her brother, Bran the Blessed, in Wales. Upon receiving the message from the starling, Bran gathers his forces to rescue Branwen, leading to a devastating war between the two countries.

---

65. Hughes, *The Book of Celtic Magic*, 160–61.

In Welsh tradition, starlings symbolise communication, freedom, and resourcefulness. Branwen's starling exemplifies the idea of finding hope in small, seemingly powerless forms, with the bird acting as a bridge between Branwen's isolation and her kin's eventual rescue mission. In this way, the starling's journey represents the power of resilience and the ingenuity required to overcome oppression. The starling's success in delivering Branwen's message also highlights the importance of family and loyalty, as it rekindles the bond between Branwen and Bran despite the distance and hardships separating them.[66]

In this way, the starling in Branwen's story becomes a symbol of hope and liberation in the face of adversity, embodying the idea that even the smallest messenger can bring about monumental change. There is also a nod to the connection between birds and fate, echoing the Mediterranean perspective of birds as augurs of the future.

In Action

Exploring the symbolism of birds through practical activities can deepen your understanding of the rune and its meanings. The following exercises are designed to help you engage with the themes of this rune in a hands-on way, whether through observation, movement, or creative expression. As you work through them, remain open to any insights that arise—both from the birds themselves and from your own experiences.

Bird-Watching

Spend some time outdoors observing the birds in your area. Watch how they move through the landscape—do they soar effortlessly on thermal currents, dark quickly between trees, or hop along the ground in search of food? Pay attention to their calls and songs, noting whether they sound like warnings, greetings, or territorial claims. Observe their interactions—are they solitary, moving in pairs, or gathering in flocks? Their behaviour offers insight into the rhythms of the natural world, reflecting the changing seasons, the availability of food, and even shifts in the weather.

---

66. Geddes and Grosset, *Celtic Mythology*, 242–46.

Research

If you're unfamiliar with the birds around you, take this opportunity to learn about them. Research at least five species native to your region, exploring their habits, habitats, and any folklore or symbolism associated with them. Field guides, library resources, and bird-watching apps can help with identification. You might also consider ways to create a bird-friendly environment in your yard, such as planting native flora, setting up feeders, or providing fresh water to encourage avian visitors.

Flight and Perspective

Find a high place—a hilltop, a lookout, or even a balcony—where you can observe the world from above. Take in the expanse of the landscape, the movement of people below, and the way the wind shapes the environment. Imagine seeing through the eyes of a bird, soaring effortlessly and viewing the world with a broader perspective. How does this shift in viewpoint change your thoughts or emotions? Do any insights arise about your own life? This exercise can serve as a reminder of the power of perspective, encouraging you to step back from everyday concerns and see the bigger picture.

Make Your Own Birds Stone

When you feel ready, begin the process of creating your Birds rune. First, take some time to reflect on what this rune represents to you. Consider the qualities of birds: their movement, songs, and ability to see the world from above. How does this relate to the wisdom you hope to gain from working with this rune?

Select a stone that feels fitting for this symbol. You might choose one that is particularly smooth, light in colour, or naturally shaped in a way that reminds you of flight or feathers. If you haven't gathered a stone for this rune yet, take your time in finding one that resonates with you. As with the rest of your stones, it should be comfortable to hold and in proportion to the others.

Once you have your stone, decide how you want to mark it. You may choose to paint, carve, or etch the symbol onto the surface. Whichever method you use, focus on infusing the stone with your understanding of the rune's meaning. As you work, hold the intention that this will be a tool for guidance and insight.

When your rune is complete, take a moment to sit with it in your hands. Feel its weight, its texture, and the energy it carries. You might wish to set it in a place of significance, carry it with you, or spend some time meditating with it for a few days to build a stronger connection. From here, your rune is ready to be used in the meditations for further exploration.

In Thought

Before beginning these meditations, take some time to familiarise yourself with the Birds rune earlier in this chapter. Ensure you can visualise its form clearly in your mind, as this will serve as an anchor throughout the exercises. You may wish to hold your rune stone as you meditate or place it before you as a point of focus.

The first meditation is unscripted; the second is longer and guided. Approach these meditations with an open mind, allowing the symbolism of the Birds rune to unfold through direct experience. If it helps, consider recording the second meditation so you can listen back and follow along without distraction.

Meditation 1: Exploring the Birds Stone

This meditation will help you build a connection with the image of the rune. The objective is to notice any existing concepts or associations that this rune might hold for you. By performing this exercise, you will be able to witness those ideas bubbling to the surface. Take note of anything that comes up and remember there is no right or wrong here. Spend some time recording anything that comes up in your journal when you are done.

Get into a comfortable position. Only lie down if you are able to relax without falling asleep. Whatever position you choose, ensure that your back is straight and supported.

Close your eyes and take a few calming breaths. Check in with your body, releasing any areas of tension. Let your breath dissolve and carry away any stress as your body softens and relaxes. Take a moment to settle into the exercise and set your intention to explore the symbol of this rune.

With your eyes still closed, visualise the symbol of the Birds. Hold the image clearly in your mind. Simply observe it, allowing insights to arise. What thoughts, ideas, or memories come to the surface? Do any sensations or emotions emerge? Take note of these while gently keeping your focus on the symbol.

If your attention drifts, gently guide it back to the symbol. Try to remain in this meditation for at least ten minutes.

You might like to perform this meditation several times as you work with this rune. You can also revisit it periodically to integrate new insights as your relationship grows.

Meditation 2: Meeting the Spirit of the Birds Rune

This is a more in-depth meditation. The objective here is to go on a journey to meet the spirit of the Birds rune so that you can build a relationship with it. This has two secondary benefits: The first is the ability to learn directly from the rune spirit and the second is to anchor that spirit in your rune stone. Again, you might like to record this script and play it back, perhaps with some calming music, or you can otherwise memorise the steps and walk yourself through the meditation. Be sure to leave adequate time at the marked pauses for interactions and input from beings within the meditation.

Begin by finding a comfortable position and closing your eyes. Take several deep, calming breaths, and let your body relax.

Take a deep breath in… and as you exhale, let go of any tension in your body. Allow yourself to settle into this moment, leaving behind any distractions or concerns. With each breath, feel yourself becoming more relaxed, more at ease.

Now, imagine yourself standing in a beautiful forest. The air is cool and fresh, and the sound of leaves rustling in the gentle breeze surrounds you. Sunlight filters through the canopy above, casting a soft dappled light onto the forest floor.

Take a moment to feel the soil beneath your feet. The earth is solid, grounding you. Each breath you take connects you more deeply with this peaceful place.

As you walk through the forest, you notice a large, ancient tree ahead of you. Its trunk is wide and strong, its bark thick and textured. There's something magical about this tree—it's as though it has been standing here for centuries, watching over the forest.

You feel drawn to the tree. As you get closer, you notice something remarkable: There is a doorway in the trunk of the tree. It's small and rounded, just

large enough for you to step through. The door itself is made of smooth wood, with intricate carvings that seem to shimmer slightly in the sunlight.

Take a moment to observe this doorway. What does it look like? Notice the details, the carvings, the way it feels as you gently reach out and touch it.

Now, when you're ready, place your hand on the door's handle. It opens easily, inviting you to step inside. Take a deep breath, and with your next exhale, step through the doorway.

As you pass through, you enter a new space. This place is calm and safe, a sanctuary just for you. Perhaps it's a beautiful garden, a peaceful meadow, or a cosy room—whatever feels right to you. Take a moment to explore this space. Feel the peace that surrounds you. You are safe here, and everything you need is already within you.

Breathe in deeply and let yourself relax even further. In this place, you are free from any worries or stress. Feel the calm washing over you, nurturing and restoring your mind and body.

Take some time here, in this space of peace and tranquillity. You can return to this place anytime you wish, simply by stepping through the doorway in the tree.

As you stand in your peaceful space, you feel the gentle stir of a breeze around you, light and refreshing. In the distance, you hear the soft fluttering of wings, as though something is coming your way, bringing with it the promise of new energy, ideas, or insights. As you walk toward this sound, you see a glowing symbol in the air ahead of you, shimmering with lightness and freedom.

This is the Birds rune. Its shape is fluid and dynamic, as if in constant motion, representing inspiration, the arrival of news, or the flight of ideas. Take a moment to stand before the Birds rune and observe it closely. Notice its graceful lines, its air of freedom, and the sense of openness it brings.

The Birds rune carries the energy of flight—of movement, vision, and the arrival of new thoughts and inspiration. It is the symbol of freedom of mind and spirit, inviting fresh perspectives and creative ideas into your life.

Breathe deeply, allowing the light and airy energy of the Birds rune to fill you. Feel it moving through your body, lifting your spirit, clearing away any heaviness or stagnation. You are now connected to the energy of inspiration, to the winds of change that bring new ideas and insights.

As you stand before this rune, you become aware of a presence nearby. It is the spirit of the Birds rune, a guide that embodies the energy of inspiration, creativity, and the arrival of news. This spirit moves gracefully, as light and free as a bird in flight, carrying with it the wisdom of the air, the wind, and the open sky.

The spirit may appear as a bird, a figure with wings, or simply a presence that feels like the essence of freedom and movement. Allow the spirit to take whatever form feels natural to you, without forcing an image.

As the spirit approaches, you feel its lightness and the excitement of something new on the horizon. This spirit carries with it messages, ideas, and the promise of inspiration. It is here to guide you in finding new perspectives, receiving creative insights, or welcoming fresh energy into your life.

Take a moment to connect with the spirit of the Birds rune. Feel its energy of freedom and inspiration. This spirit is here to bring you news—whether it's an idea you've been waiting for, clarity on a situation, or a new perspective on something important in your life.

The spirit now invites you to reflect on an area of your life where you seek inspiration or new ideas. Perhaps there's a project, a decision, or a creative endeavour where you feel stuck, or maybe you are simply open to receiving whatever news or guidance the spirit has to offer. When you are ready, silently or aloud, ask the spirit of the Birds rune to bring you inspiration, to help you see things from a new angle, or to offer you fresh insights.

(Pause for reflection, to ask and connect.)

The spirit may respond with feelings of excitement, images of new possibilities, or a clear sense of direction. It might show you a new idea or help you understand something in a different way. Trust whatever comes to you, even if it feels subtle or fleeting. The Birds rune reminds us that inspiration can arrive on the wings of the wind, sometimes in whispers, sometimes in sudden flashes of clarity.

Take a moment to sit with the guidance you've received. Feel how the energy of the Birds rune opens your mind and spirit to new possibilities, bringing a sense of lightness and excitement to your path.

Now, the spirit offers you a final gift—a message, a symbol, or a piece of inspiration that you can carry with you as you move forward. Open your heart and mind to receive this gift of insight.

(Pause briefly to receive the message.)

As your time with the spirit of the Birds rune comes to an end, you feel a deep sense of gratitude. The spirit begins to lift, just as a bird rises into the air, but the feeling of inspiration remains, filling the space with lightness, clarity, and the promise of new ideas to come.

Take a deep breath, knowing that you can return to this space and this spirit whenever you seek inspiration or new perspectives. The energy of the Birds rune is always within you, ready to lift your spirit and bring you the guidance you need.

Now, turn away from the rune and begin to walk back toward the doorway in the tree. As you move through your peaceful space, you carry the lightness of the Birds rune with you, knowing that its energy will continue to bring you fresh ideas and inspiration.

Step through the doorway once again, returning to the forest. Feel the gentle breeze around you, hear the distant call of birds in the trees, and sense the calmness of the forest as you return to the present.

With each breath, bring yourself back to the present moment. Begin to notice your body again, feeling the surface beneath you, the air on your skin.

When you are ready, gently open your eyes, feeling light, inspired, and connected to the energy of the Birds rune.

Take a moment to record your insights: What did you see? What have you learnt? Did anything surprise you? As part of your records, you can sketch out any particularly vivid imagery that came through your meditation as a way of grounding it into the physical world.

You might also like to try a grounding exercise to help bring you back to the present moment. This can be achieved by standing barefoot on the earth, imagining energetic roots reaching from your feet into the ground and balancing your energy, or resting your forehead on the floor for a moment.

In Words

Journaling can help solidify your understanding of the Birds rune, allowing you to track your evolving relationship with its symbolism. Begin by noting any key points from your research—what stood out to you about birds in mythology, folklore, or nature? Were there any surprising connections or recurring themes?

Reflect on your personal relationship with birds. What do they mean to you? Have you had any memorable encounters with them in your daily life or dreams? Consider whether different birds evoke distinct emotions or ideas. A soaring eagle might inspire a sense of freedom and power, while a gathering of crows could suggest mystery, wisdom, or even a warning.

Now, compare your impressions of birds in general with the energy of the Birds rune itself. Do they align, or does the rune convey something different? How does working with the rune shift your perspective on birds and their symbolism?

Finally, take all of these reflections and attempt to define the meaning of the Birds rune in your own words. Rather than relying solely on traditional interpretations, let your personal experiences guide your understanding. This exercise will deepen your connection to the rune and help you integrate its wisdom into your practice.

Chapter Eight
The Waves Stone

The Waves rune symbolises movement, change, and the flow of life's journeys. It represents both physical travel and inner transformation, reflecting the ever-shifting nature of emotions, experiences, and personal growth. Like the tide, it speaks to cycles of departure and return, urging one to embrace the unknown and navigate life's currents with adaptability.

The Waves stone usually depicts either independent spirals or the stereotypical two-dimensional sketched water to represent waves. In the case of the latter, it can sometimes be confused with the Birds stone to the unwary new reader. Ashcroft-Nowicki's original article displayed the Waves as five small spirals. Crowther's was one blue wave spiralling in on itself. By the early 2000s, West was writing about this rune as being a blue snake rather than a wave, though her divinatory associations with the stone remain very similar to earlier iterations.[67]

In a Reading

The spiralling waters of the Waves stone represent movement of many different kinds. In our physical journeys as well as journeys more personal and inner facing, this stone reminds us to be fluid and adaptive in the face of change. Waves are a visible form of water in motion; as such, this rune represents movement. The waves lapping at the shores of our homelands are formed of the same water

67. West, *The Real Witches' Book of Spells and Rituals*, 153.

that connects (and separates) all lands. It is here that we gain the interpretation of travel or journeys. Journeys by boat were a significant part of the history of human cultures and also played a role in the history of this divination system. An alternative name given to this rune by Crowther is the Relatives rune.[68]

The Waves rune speaks to the state of flowing like water, or otherwise advises us to do so, as well as the yearning for things far off or the call to move forward. It encapsulates movement itself but also those forces that move us.

In Culture and Mythology

Waves, with their endless motion and transformative power, serve as symbols of life's fundamental forces—change, emotion, destruction, creation, and the unknown. They reflect the rhythms of nature, the depths of the subconscious, and the constant push and pull between order and chaos in human existence. Whether representing spiritual journeys, emotional states, or cosmic cycles, waves carry deep significance in the mythologies and folklore of cultures around the world.

Odysseus

In Homer's *The Odyssey*, the sea and its waves are central to Odysseus's journey, symbolising the trials he faces. Poseidon, god of the sea, stirs the waves to challenge Odysseus, who must struggle against the unknown forces of the ocean to return home.[69] The relentless waves serve as metaphors for fate and the uncontrollable forces that guide human destiny.

Emotions and the Subconscious

Waves have long been used as metaphors for emotions, particularly those that are overwhelming, unpredictable, or ever-changing, such as fear, love, grief, and passion. Just as the sea can be calm one moment and stormy the next, human emotions ebb and flow, sometimes gently lapping at the shore of consciousness and other times surging forth with the power of a tempest. This connection between water and emotion is found across many cultures, reinforcing the idea that deep feelings, like the ocean, can be both beautiful and treacherous.

---

68. Crowther, *Lid Off the Cauldron*, 111.
69. Fry, *Troy*, 152–57.

In European folklore and beyond, the sea is often personified by mermaids, sirens, and other water spirits who emerge from the waves, symbolising the mysterious and sometimes perilous allure of the emotional and subconscious realms. These beings are frequently depicted as both enchanting and dangerous, reflecting the dual nature of human emotions—their ability to inspire and uplift as well as to consume and destroy.

One well-known example is the Greek Sirens, who, though sometimes depicted as birdlike creatures, are associated with the sea. Their hauntingly beautiful songs lure sailors to their doom, much like how unchecked emotions can lead one astray. In *The Odyssey*, Odysseus famously had himself tied to the mast of his ship so he could hear the Sirens' song without succumbing to their pull, while his crew plugged their ears with beeswax. This myth serves as a powerful metaphor for the need to balance emotional depth with reason and control.

A similar theme appears in German folklore with Lorelei, a beautiful spectral woman said to dwell atop a cliff overlooking the Rhine River. Her song is so mesmerising that it causes sailors to lose focus, steering their ships into the rocks below. Like the Sirens, Lorelei embodies the seduction and destructive nature of unchecked emotions, particularly longing, sorrow, and obsession.

Beyond Western traditions, many cultures feature water spirits that reflect the powerful emotional symbolism of waves. In Japanese folklore, the Nure-onna, a serpentlike water spirit with the face of a woman, is said to appear near bodies of water, sometimes helping or deceiving those who encounter her, much like shifting emotions that can be either beneficial or overwhelming.

These stories collectively reinforce the idea that waves, like emotions, are an unstoppable and natural force. They can be navigated but never truly controlled. To ride the waves of feeling is to embrace the unpredictable, to respect the depths, and to learn when to surrender and when to steer towards calmer waters.

Poseidon

The Greek god Poseidon, ruler of the sea, has absolute control over the waves, shaping the fates of sailors, lands, and even entire kingdoms. In moments of anger, he can unleash tempests, causing shipwrecks, storms, and even earthquakes—his wrath famously turning the tides of mythological stories. One such example is found in *The Odyssey*, where Poseidon relentlessly torments Odysseus for blinding his son, the Cyclops Polyphemus. Enraged, the sea god raises violent storms, wrecks Odysseus's ships, and prolongs his journey home for years, making the ocean an ever-present force of challenge and transformation.

Yet Poseidon is not solely a destroyer; his domain also provides sustenance, trade, and passage between lands. Coastal cities thrive due to the riches of the sea, and fishermen rely on its bounty for survival. Poseidon's favour can grant smooth sailing, prosperity, and discovery, showing how the ocean embodies both the peril and promise of the unknown. This duality—of creation and destruction, of safe passage and deadly storm—reflects the deeper symbolism of the sea itself, a vast and uncontrollable force that mirrors the ever-changing nature of life.[70]

Viking Culture

The sea and its waves held great significance for the Vikings, whose seafaring lifestyle was central to their culture and survival. The ocean was both a pathway to new lands and a treacherous force, embodying the unpredictable nature of fate itself. For the Vikings, waves could symbolise the ebb and flow of destiny, with the sea representing the vast, unknown future.

Norse mythology reflects this deep connection to the sea in numerous ways. The Aegir, a powerful Jotun associated with the ocean, is both a giver of bounty and a bringer of doom. He is said to host great feasts for the gods in his underwater hall, serving endless ale from a massive cauldron, yet he also commands the waves and is feared for his ability to drag ships and sailors to their deaths.[71] His nine daughters, the billow maidens, each represent a different kind of wave, reinforcing the idea that the sea was a living, shifting force, both beautiful and perilous.

Another well-known tale is that of Thor's fishing expedition, where he sought to catch the monstrous Midgard Serpent, Jörmungandr, a creature so vast it encircles the world. As Thor rowed out into the stormy ocean with the giant Hymir, he baited his line with an ox's head and managed to hook the great serpent. The sea churned violently as Jörmungandr thrashed, pulling at the line, and Thor's battle with the creature embodied the raw, uncontrollable power of the ocean itself. Though Thor nearly succeeded in slaying the serpent, Hymir, fearing the

70. Fry, *Mythos: The Illustrated Story*, 78–79.
71. Lafayllve, *A Practical Heathen's Guide to Asatru*, 47.

consequences, cut the line, allowing Jörmungandr to slip back into the depths.[72] This story highlights the Norse view of the sea as a domain of chaos and primal forces, where even gods struggle to assert control.

Beyond mythology, the Vikings themselves saw the sea as both a means of prosperity and a constant challenge. Their sagas tell of perilous voyages, where warriors braved towering waves and storms, uncertain whether they would reach new lands or be swallowed by the abyss. This constant risk reinforced their belief in wyrd, the Norse concept of fate. Like the ocean, life was unpredictable, and one could only strive to meet it with courage.

Celtic Folklore

In Celtic culture, water—especially the ever-moving waves of the sea—is seen as a boundary between worlds. The ceaseless motion of waves mirrors the fluid transition between different states of being, symbolising the passage between life and death, the conscious and unconscious mind, and the physical and spiritual realms. Bodies of water were seen as liminal spaces, places where one could encounter the Otherworld, communicate with spirits, or receive divine inspiration.

One striking example of this belief is the myth of Tír na nóg, the fabled Land of Youth. In Irish mythology, Tír na nóg is an ethereal, otherworldly paradise said to exist beyond the western sea. It is a place of eternal beauty, where time moves differently, and those who enter may never return to the mortal world unchanged. The most famous story associated with Tír na nóg is that of Oisín, a warrior-poet of the Fianna, who falls in love with Niamh, a woman from the Otherworld. She arrives on a white horse, crossing the waves to bring him back to her realm. Oisín lives in bliss for what seems like a few years, but when he finally returns to Ireland, he discovers that centuries have passed.[73] The waves, in this tale, act as the threshold between mortal life and the timeless existence of the Otherworld.

Similarly, sacred wells, rivers, and coastal regions were often associated with gods, spirits, and portals to the Divine. The Boyne River, named after the goddess Boann, was believed to hold mystical power and wisdom. The river itself was formed when Boann, defying sacred laws, approached the Well of Segais, a source of ultimate knowledge. When she attempted to drink from it, the waters rose in

---

72. Crawford, *The Poetic Edda*, 91–99.
73. Geddes and Grosset, *Celtic Mythology*, 167–84.

a great flood, creating the river and dispersing its wisdom throughout the land.[74] This story underscores the idea that water, particularly flowing water, serves as a link between realms, carrying hidden knowledge and spiritual transformation.

Waves also held significance in Celtic seafaring traditions, where the ocean presented not only a physical challenge but also a spiritual journey. Sailors and warriors would often seek omens in the movement of the waves, interpreting them as messages from the gods or ancestors. The sea was seen as a living force, unpredictable and powerful, capable of granting passage or swallowing ships whole.

Through these myths and traditions, the Celtic cultures recognised waves as more than just a physical phenomenon—they were messengers of fate, boundaries between the known and unknown, and guides on the journey between different states of existence.

The River Styx

The River Styx in Greek mythology is one of the five rivers of the Underworld and is known as the river of hatred. Flowing around Hades nine times, it separates the world of the living from the dead, and its waters are both sacred and perilous. According to myth, the gods swear binding oaths upon the Styx, and to break such an oath would bring divine punishment.[75] This solemn pact reflects the river's role as a boundary and its deep connection to the forces of fate and justice.

The Styx symbolises the inevitability of death and the passage into the unknown, encapsulating the barrier between life and the eternal mysteries beyond. It represents the fearsome and transformative power of death as well as the profound reverence and caution with which ancient cultures approached the idea of an afterlife. By swearing on the Styx, the gods themselves acknowledged its greater, immutable authority—a force even they could not defy.

In a broader sense, the Styx serves as a reminder of the respect due to life's darker mysteries. It stands as a river of transition, a powerful symbol of boundaries and unbreakable vows, reminding us of the irreversible nature of certain choices and the sacred weight of promises that bind both mortals and immortals

---

74. Geddes and Grosset, *Celtic Mythology*, 49–50.
75. Fry, *Mythos*, 285.

alike. It also speaks poetically to the transformative power of journeys or travel. To cross the River Styx is to be completely and irrevocably changed.

In Action

The following activities are designed to help you explore and connect with water in your landscape and through an embodied experience.

Ocean Observation

Take a trip to the ocean if you can and spend some time immersing your senses in this marvellous companion and teacher. Watch the way it moves, smell it in the air, and feel the way it flavours the winds. Close your eyes and listen to the sounds it makes, ebbing and flowing, like the breathing of a Titan. Notice the way the ocean has carved the coastline, and think of the effortless force of the waves. Note what else comes to mind as you let the water fill your senses.

If you cannot visit the ocean, you can try a river instead. Failing that, close your eyes and try to recall the experience of waves and water with as many of your senses as possible. You can do this while in the shower if it helps. Hold this and notice what arises for you.

Create a Map

Research the waterways in your area and develop an awareness of how water shapes the land and the life that depends on it. Where does your water come from? Does it originate from a nearby river, a network of underground springs, or a distant reservoir? Consider the natural flow of water in your surroundings—are there creeks winding through your local landscape, freshwater springs bubbling up from the earth, or estuaries where freshwater and saltwater meet? If you live near the ocean, reflect on how the tides shape the coastline and influence the climate and wildlife of your region.

Despite their natural beauty, waterways often face significant environmental challenges. Investigate the state of the water around you—is it clean and healthy, or does it suffer from pollution, overuse, or the impact of urban development? Are local rivers prone to drying up, or do they flood unpredictably? If you live in an area with heavy industry or agriculture, how do these activities affect the water supply? Some communities battle contamination from chemicals, sewage runoff, or plastic waste, while others struggle with drought and the depletion of freshwater sources.

Understanding the condition of your local water sources connects you more deeply to the land and its cycles. If possible, visit a local river, creek, or lake and observe its movement, its colour, and the life it supports. Are there fish, birds, or other animals that rely on this water? Does it feel vibrant and thriving, or does it carry signs of distress, such as algal blooms, litter, or an unnatural stillness?

By learning about the waterways in your area, you gain insight into the role they play in both the natural and the human world. This awareness fosters a stronger relationship with the element of water—not just as a concept but as a living presence that sustains ecosystems, shapes landscapes, and supports daily life. Using the information you gather, create a map that traces the waterways around you, marking their paths through the landscape. Let this map be more than just a guide—let it be a record of connection, a way of deepening your relationship with the living currents that shape your environment.

Get to Know Your Local Water Spirits

Once your map is complete, set out to visit as many of these sites as you can. Approach each one with curiosity and reverence, taking the time to observe not just the physical characteristics of the place—the movement of the water, the plant life at its edge, the quality of the air—but also the way it makes you feel. Does it seem still and reflective, rushing and restless, or heavy with history?

As you stand by the water, take note of what rises within you. What thoughts, emotions, or memories surface as you listen to the sounds of the waves, the gurgling of a stream, or the hush of still water? Some places may feel vibrant and full of life, while others may carry a sense of sorrow or neglect. Do certain locations feel connected, as if they share a thread of energy despite the distance between them? If you return to the same place on different days, do you notice changes—perhaps a shift in the mood of the water, the way it interacts with the wind, or the life it attracts?

As an act of reciprocity, consider making a small offering at each site. This could be as simple as clearing up rubbish left behind by others, participating in a local waterway regeneration project, or making a symbolic gesture—leaving a biodegradable token of appreciation or whispering words of gratitude. Honouring these places, even in small ways, strengthens your bond with them and builds the awareness that your presence is part of the landscape, not separate from it.

Make Your Own Waves Stone

With your reflections in mind, turn to the next step of your journey: crafting your waves rune. The first step is to find the right stone—one that speaks to you. It may be smooth and waterworn, pulled from the bed of a stream or the shore of a lake, or perhaps a rougher piece of earth that carries the story of the land. Take your time in choosing. Walk along the water's edge or through places where the tides have shaped the landscape. When you find a stone that feels right, hold it in your hands. Notice its texture, its weight. Does it remind you of the movement of water? Does it seem to hum with quiet potential?

Carry the stone with you for a time before marking it. Let it settle into your pocket, your palm, your daily life. Feel its presence as a quiet companion, a piece of the landscape now walking beside you. During this time, reflect on the lessons of water—the way it moves effortlessly around obstacles, the way it carves through rock over time, the way it can be both gentle and fierce. Let these reflections deepen your connection to the rune you are about to create.

When the moment feels right, mark your stone with the symbol of the Waves rune. Choose a method that resonates with you. You might carve it carefully with a fine tool, etch it with a heated point, or paint it in flowing strokes. However you choose to inscribe it, let your actions be deliberate and focused. As you work, hold in your mind all that you have learnt—the rivers and streams, the shifting tides, the unseen currents that shape the world. This is more than just a craft; it is an act of intention, a way to bring the wisdom of water into physical form.

Once your rune is complete, take a moment to sit with it. Feel the weight of it in your hands, the texture beneath your fingers. In the small but potent symbol, you hold the essence of movement, transformation, and the deep unseen connections that link all things. Let it serve as a reminder of the ever-flowing nature of life and the lessons the waves have taught you.

In Thought

Before beginning the following meditations, take some time to familiarise yourself with the Waves rune symbol earlier in this chapter. Study it carefully until you can clearly visualise it with your eyes closed. Once you feel confident in your mental image of the rune, you are ready to proceed with the first meditation. For the second meditation, you may find it helpful to record yourself reading the script, allowing you to listen and follow along, or alternatively, you can memorise the narrative and follow it at your own pace.

Meditation 1: Exploring the Waves Stone

The following simple meditation will help you build a connection with the image of the rune. The objective is to notice any existing concepts or associations that this rune might hold for you. By performing this exercise, you will be able to witness those ideas bubbling to the surface. Take note of anything that comes up and remember there is no right or wrong here. Spend some time recording anything that comes up in your journal when you are done.

Get into a comfortable position. Only lie down if you are able to relax without falling asleep. Whatever position you choose, ensure that your back is straight and supported.

Close your eyes. Take several calming breaths, checking in with your body and relaxing any tension. Let your breath carry away stress as you soften and relax. Spend a minute settling into the exercise and set the intention to explore the symbol of this rune.

With your eyes still closed, visualise the symbol of the Waves clearly in your mind. Simply regard the symbol and remain open to insights. Note any thoughts, ideas, or memories that arise, as well as any body sensations. Keep your attention gently focused on the symbol of the Waves.

If your focus wanders, gently bring it back to the symbol. Aim to stay in this meditation for at least ten minutes.

You may wish to repeat this meditation several times as you work with this rune. You can also revisit it periodically to integrate new insights as your relationship develops.

Meditation 2: Meeting the Spirit of the Waves Rune

This is a guided meditation. The objective here is to go on a journey to meet the spirit of the Waves rune so that you can build a relationship with it. This has two secondary benefits: The first is the ability to learn directly from the rune spirit, and the second is to anchor that spirit in your rune stone. You might like to record this script and play it back, perhaps with some calming music, or otherwise memorise the steps and walk yourself through the meditation. Be sure to leave adequate time at the marked pauses for interactions and input from beings within the meditation.

Begin by finding a comfortable position and closing your eyes. Take several deep, calming breaths, and let your body relax.

Take a deep breath in … and as you exhale, let go of any tension in your body. Allow yourself to settle into this moment, leaving behind any distractions or concerns. With each breath, feel yourself becoming more relaxed, more at ease.

Now, imagine yourself standing in a beautiful forest. The air is cool and fresh, and the sound of leaves rustling in the gentle breeze surrounds you. Sunlight filters through the canopy above, casting a soft dappled light onto the forest floor.

Take a moment to feel the soil beneath your feet. The earth is solid, grounding you. Each breath you take connects you more deeply with this peaceful place.

As you walk through the forest, you notice a large, ancient tree ahead of you. Its trunk is wide and strong, its bark thick and textured. There's something magical about this tree—it's as though it has been standing here for centuries, watching over the forest.

You feel drawn to the tree. As you get closer, you notice something remarkable: There is a doorway in the trunk of the tree. It's small and rounded, just large enough for you to step through. The door itself is made of smooth wood, with intricate carvings that seem to shimmer slightly in the sunlight.

Take a moment to observe this doorway. What does it look like? Notice the details, the carvings, the way it feels as you gently reach out and touch it.

Now, when you're ready, place your hand on the door's handle. It opens easily, inviting you to step inside. Take a deep breath, and with your next exhale, step through the doorway.

As you pass through, you enter a new space. This place is calm and safe, a sanctuary just for you. Perhaps it's a beautiful garden, a peaceful meadow, or a cosy room—whatever feels right to you. Take a moment to explore this space. Feel the peace that surrounds you. You are safe here, and everything you need is already within you.

Breathe in deeply, and let yourself relax even further. In this place, you are free from any worries or stress. Feel the calm washing over you, nurturing and restoring your mind and body.

Take some time here, in this space of peace and tranquillity. You can return to this place anytime you wish, simply by stepping through the doorway in the tree.

As you stand in your peaceful space, you notice a sound in the distance—soft and rhythmic, like the gentle lapping of waves against the shore. The air around you seems to move, flowing in a calm yet powerful rhythm, guiding you forward. As you follow this sensation, you see a soft glow ahead, shimmering with fluid, flowing energy.

This is the Waves rune, and as you approach, you can see its form—a pattern that rises and falls like the rhythm of the ocean. The energy of this rune moves like water, representing the power of movement and journeys—both physical and spiritual. It speaks to the flow of life, the unfolding of paths, and the natural currents that guide us forward.

Take a moment to stand before the Waves rune, feeling its gentle, flowing energy. Notice how it ebbs and flows, always in motion, shifting and changing. The Waves rune serves as a reminder that life itself is a journey: Movement, whether through change or growth, is a natural part of that journey.

Breathe deeply, allowing the energy of the Waves rune to wash over you. Feel its flowing movement enter your body, bringing with it a sense of progress, direction, and forward motion. You are connected to the energy of motion and the currents that guide you on your path.

Standing in this peaceful place, you become aware of another presence nearby. This is the spirit of the Waves rune, a guide who embodies the essence of movement and journeys. The spirit approaches with the grace and power of flowing water, with an aura that feels both soothing and dynamic, encapsulating the wisdom of the tides, the rivers, and the paths that unfold before you.

The spirit of the Waves rune may appear as a figure formed of water, a shimmering entity, or an energy that feels fluid and constantly moving. Allow the spirit to come to you however feels natural. Do not force an image.

As the spirit draws near, you are overcome with a sense of calm yet purposeful movement. This spirit is here to guide you on your journey, help you understand the changes and transitions you may be experiencing, and support you as you move forward in life.

Take a moment to connect with the spirit. Note the feeling of its energy: the energy of flow and movement. Notice the way it carries with it the knowledge of journeys—physical, emotional, or spiritual. This spirit embodies the knowledge that life is in constant motion, and the journey itself is just as important as the destination.

The spirit invites you to reflect on an area of your life where you are experiencing movement or change. Perhaps you are on a journey of personal growth, or maybe there's some transition or decision ahead of you. Reflect on where you are in this journey. When you are ready, silently or aloud, ask the spirit for guidance. Ask for help navigating the currents of life, understanding the direction you are heading, or to find peace within the movement and change.

(Pause for reflection.)

You may receive your answer as feelings, images, or a sense of knowing. The spirit could show you the path ahead, reveal a new direction, or help you to understand the natural flow of the experience you brought forward. Trust whatever comes to you. The Waves rune teaches us that movement is not always predictable. It simply is.

Sit with the guidance. Notice the way the energy of the Waves rune brings clarity about the path ahead, helping you embrace movement and changes in your life and revealing how you are being carried forward toward growth and understanding.

Now, the spirit offers you a final message—a gift of insight or support on your path. Open yourself to receiving this message.

(Pause briefly to receive the message.)

As your time with the spirit of the Waves rune comes to an end, you feel a deep sense of peace and gratitude. The spirit begins to fade like the retreating tide, but the flowing energy of the Waves rune remains, filling the space with calm motion.

Take a deep breath, knowing that you can return to this space and this spirit whenever you seek guidance or clarity on your journey. The energy of the Waves rune is always within you. It is in the currents of life, helping you move forward with grace and purpose.

Now, turn away from the rune and begin to walk back toward the doorway in the tree. As you move through your peaceful space, you carry everything you learnt and experienced here with you.

Step through the doorway once again and return to the forest. Feel the ground beneath your feet. Hear the soft rustling of the leaves in the wind and sense the peaceful energy of the forest around you.

With each breath, bring yourself back to the present moment. Begin to notice your body again, the sensations of your seat, the sounds of the air, the temperature.

When you are ready, gently open your eyes, feeling calm, empowered, and connected to the movement of life.

When you have finished, take a moment to record your insights: What did you see? What have you learnt? Did anything surprise you? As part of your records, you can sketch out any particularly vivid imagery that came through your meditation as a way of grounding it into the physical world.

You might also like to try a grounding exercise to help bring you back to the present moment. This can be achieved by standing barefoot on the earth, imagining energetic roots reaching from your feet into the ground and balancing your energy, or resting your forehead on the floor for a moment.

In Words

As you reflect on your experiences with the Waves rune, take time to write down your thoughts, feelings, and insights from all the work with the Waves rune symbol. Use the following prompts to guide your journaling and deepen your understanding.

Have your ideas about waves and water shifted through these exercises and meditations? What new aspects of water have you discovered? Consider how the symbolism of water—as both gentle and powerful, constant and ever-changing—might relate to your own life and experiences.

Was there anything that particularly took you by surprise or stood out to you while working with this rune? Perhaps a specific moment in the meditation or a detail in the symbolism of the waves resonated deeply. Write about what felt significant and why.

Waves are symbols of movement, transformation, and flow. How do you see these qualities in your own life right now? Are there any areas where you're experiencing change, challenge, or growth? How might the energy of waves offer insight or support in navigating these changes?

In your own words, take time to record your understanding of the Waves rune's significance. What does it mean to you? How do the waves reflect aspects of your personal journey, whether related to emotional, physical, or spiritual movement? Consider how this rune might guide or influence you moving forward.

Reflect on the role water has as a boundary between realms—the physical and spiritual, life and death, conscious and unconscious. How do you see water playing a role as a bridge or divider in your life? Is there something you're currently crossing, or a transition you are navigating?

What personal experiences or memories do you have with water? How have these experiences shaped your relationship with the element of water? Reflect on how your connection to water deepens or shifts as you engage with the Waves rune.

After working with the Waves rune, how do you feel about the broader symbolism of water in your life? Do you feel more connected to the natural flow of things or perhaps more aware of areas where you resist change or movement? Take time to write down any final reflections, focusing on the lessons the Waves rune has brought to you.

By writing down your insights and experiences, you solidify the symbolic meanings of the Waves rune in your life and deepen your connection to its transformative power. This practice of reflection can help integrate the wisdom of the water element allowing you to move forward with greater clarity and understanding.

Chapter Nine
The Wheat Stone

The Wheat rune displays a sheaf of wheat, either harvested or ripe and ready to harvest. The original illustration accompanying Ashcroft-Nowicki's 1977 article shows a Wheat stone with five stalks. Crowther called this the Lucky stone and described it as a single ear of corn.[76]

Whether it depicts the wheat as harvested or ripe and ready to harvest, the Wheat stone speaks of the tangible rewards associated with hard work and sacrifice. It can also represent the fruits of the harvest itself, and it speaks of abundance for those willing to work for it.

In a Reading

In a divinatory reading, the Wheat rune, which Ashcroft-Nowicki called the Stone of Harvest, embodies the dual nature of reward and sacrifice associated with labour. It signifies not only the tangible rewards for physical work—the bountiful harvest reaped from diligent effort—but the very essence of what is being harvested. This rune reflects the fruits of one's work, highlighting the importance of perseverance and dedication in achieving one's goals.

However, it also serves as a reminder that with every harvest comes an element of sacrifice; the act of cultivation requires not only effort but also the relinquishing

76. Crowther, *Lid Off the Cauldron*, 112.

of resources, time, and sometimes even personal desires. Thus, the Wheat rune encourages reflection on the balance between what is gained and what must be given up to achieve true abundance.

In Culture and Mythology

Wheat and grain hold profound symbolism in folklore and mythology, often representing fertility, abundance, and the cyclical nature of life. These grains have been central to human existence for thousands of years, making them powerful symbols in various cultural narratives. In the following section, we will explore some of these concepts to begin developing an understanding of the Wheat rune.

Agricultural Society

Wheat is a powerful symbol of life-sustaining abundance in many agrarian cultures, representing the earth's fertility and the nourishment provided by the harvest. Its cultivation has long been central to human survival, making it a potent emblem of prosperity, sustenance, and the rhythms of nature. The cycle of sowing, growing, and reaping wheat mirrors the broader cycle of life—birth, growth, death, and renewal—making it a recurring motif in mythology, folklore, and ritual.

In ancient Greece, wheat was closely associated with Demeter, the goddess of agriculture and the harvest, whose name is often translated as "corn mother" or "barley mother."[77] The Eleusinian Mysteries, one of the most sacred rites of the ancient world, were centred around Demeter and her daughter, Persephone.[78] The myth of Persephone's descent into the Underworld will be explored more fully further in this chapter.

Similarly, in Egyptian mythology, wheat was linked to Osiris, the god of fertility, death, and resurrection. According to myth, Osiris was killed and dismembered, his body scattered across the land. His resurrection was often associated with the annual flooding of the Nile, which replenished the soil and ensured a bountiful harvest.[79] Wheat was a key crop sustained by these floods, and its growth served as a tangible expression of Osiris's rebirth, reinforcing its role as a

77. Fry, *Mythos*, 80.
78. Clinch, "Ecstasy and Initiation in the Eleusinian Mysteries," 314–31.
79. Editors of Encyclopaedia Britannica, "Osiris."

symbol of both mortality and renewal. Its use in certain rituals is outlined in the "Grains of Osiris" section of this chapter.

In Christianity, bread made from wheat is central to the Eucharist, symbolising the body of Christ and the idea of spiritual nourishment. The grain must be crushed and transformed into flour before becoming bread, echoing themes of sacrifice, transformation, and sustenance. This imagery underscores wheat's connection to both physical and spiritual life, making it a deeply layered symbol of abundance, death, and renewal.

John Barleycorn

John Barleycorn is a character and symbolic figure from British and Scottish folklore, representing the spirit of the grain, particularly barley, and the cycle of the agricultural year. He is often associated with the production of beer and whiskey, as barley is a key ingredient in both. John Barleycorn embodies the idea of death and rebirth through the harvesting of grain and is celebrated in songs, poems, and traditions as a symbol of both human labour and the gifts of nature.[80] The most famous account of John Barleycorn appears in the traditional ballad of the same name, which has been sung for centuries in Britain. The ballad describes the personification of barley and how he suffers at the hands of farmers, ultimately transforming and living on through the products the farmers make from him.

Grains of Osiris

The grain symbol also figures in the story of Osiris, the Egyptian god of the afterlife, who is killed and resurrected. Osiris is often depicted with wheat growing from his body, symbolising regeneration and life emerging from death.[81] At the temple of Mendes, figures of Osiris were made from a wheat dough containing whole seeds. These figures were then ritually buried in the temple, where the seeds would then sprout, representing the resurrection of the god.[82]

80. "Who is John Barleycorn? Gruesome Origins and Modern Retellings," *Arcane Alchemy* (blog).
81. Ragueh, "The Blessing of Grain Represented in God 'Nepri' and His Affiliate Gods of Grain," 1–22.
82. Editors of Encyclopaedia Britannica, "Osiris."

Demeter and Persephone

In Greek mythology, wheat is closely associated with Demeter, the goddess of the harvest, and her Roman counterpart, Ceres. Persephone, Demeter's daughter, was gathering flowers when she was abducted by Hades, the god of the Underworld. In her grief, Demeter abandoned her duties, causing the earth to wither and crops to fail. Famine spread until Zeus intervened, decreeing that Persephone could return—so long as she had not eaten in the Underworld. However, she had consumed six pomegranate seeds, binding her to Hades for six months of the year. As a result, she spent the barren winter months in the Underworld, while her return in spring brought renewal and the flourishing of crops, mirroring the agricultural cycle of wheat and the rhythms of life and death.[83]

Grains and Wealth

In ancient Egypt, grain was so vital that it was used as currency, with workers and artisans often paid in rations of bread and beer made from wheat and barley. Pharaohs built vast granaries to store surplus grain, ensuring stability during times of drought or famine.[84] Similarly, in Mesopotamia, temples controlled large grain reserves, which functioned as both religious offerings and economic assets, supporting the link between agriculture, divine favour, and societal wealth.[85] In Rome, wheat was central to the *annona*, a state-sponsored grain distribution system that provided free or subsidised bread to citizens, demonstrating how grain symbolised both prosperity and political power.[86] Even in medieval Europe, grain was a measure of a lord's wealth, with vast fields of wheat signifying dominance and security, as grain could be stored, traded, or used to sustain armies.[87] Across cultures, wheat remained a powerful symbol of stability, abundance, and the prosperity of a people.

---

83. Fry, *Mythos*, 181–85.
84. Signorelli, "The Power of Grain."
85. Newman, "The History of Grain Storage."
86. Erdkamp, Paul, "annona (grain)," *Oxford Classical Dictionary*, accessed March 2025, https://oxfordre.com/classics/view/10.1093/acrefore/9780199381135.001.0001/acrefore-9780199381135-e-8000.
87. Hybel, "The Grain Trade in Northern Europe Before 1350," 219–47.

European Folk Customs

In European folklore, wheat and grain were not only essential for sustenance. They also played a role in spiritual and magical traditions. In England and Scotland, corn dollies—woven figures made from the last sheaf of wheat—were crafted at harvest time to house the spirit of the grain, ensuring the land's fertility for the coming year. These figures were often kept through the winter and then ploughed back into the fields in spring to bless the new crop.[88]

In Slavic traditions, a similar belief existed in the form of the Rye Mother or Wheat Bride, where the last sheaf of grain was dressed and honoured as the embodiment of the field's vitality. This sheaf was sometimes placed in the home or a communal space as a charm for abundance and protection.[89]

The Bavarian *erntekrone* (harvest crown), a wreath of woven wheat, rye, or barley, was paraded through villages and hung in homes or barns to ensure good fortune and prosperity. In some regions of Britain, France, and Germany, farmers would sprinkle wheat grains around their homes or barns to ward off evil spirits and bring blessings upon their household.[90]

These customs reflect the deep connection between grain and the cycles of life, protection, and renewal, indicating wheat's role as a sacred and life-giving force in agrarian societies.

Modern Paganism and Witchcraft

In modern Pagan festivals, particularly those tied to the changing of the seasons, such as Lughnasadh (often called Lammas in some traditions), wheat plays a significant role as a symbol of the earth's fertility and the deep connection between humans and the land. Lughnasadh marks the first grain harvest of the year, and it is a celebration of abundance, gratitude, and the cycles of life and death that govern nature. The cutting of the first sheaf of wheat is often viewed as a sacred act, symbolising not only the culmination of the earth's fertile work but also the need for sacrifice in order to sustain life.

Wheat, and grain generally, is revered not just as food but as a bridge between the physical world and the spiritual realm. Historically, the harvest of grain was

---

88. Opie and Tatem, *A Dictionary of Superstitions*, 96.
89. "Old-Slavic Symbolism of Bread and Harvest Rituals in Poland."
90. Opie and Tatem, *A Dictionary of Superstitions*, 441.

vital for survival, and its sanctity was recognised in many cultures. Today, in modern Paganism, bread made from freshly harvested wheat is often used in rituals, representing sustenance, prosperity, and the cycle of growth and decay. It's common to bake a loaf of bread or cakes for offerings during Lammas celebrations, sometimes even sharing them with the community as a reminder of the interconnectedness of all beings.

The act of preparing and consuming bread also carries symbolic weight. As the grain is transformed into something nourishing, it reflects the transformation that occurs within us and within the cycles of nature. Whether it is shaped into traditional round loaves or carved into intricate symbols, bread holds both a practical and a spiritual significance during Lammas. It is served as a reminder of the harvest's bounty, the work required to produce it, and the cycles of death and rebirth that sustain life.

In modern practices, Lammas rituals often involve the sharing of bread or grain-based foods in a communal feast, honouring the harvest and giving thanks for the earth's generosity. Some Pagans may even perform a symbolic "bread blessing," acknowledging the earth's gifts and reaffirming their bond with the land.[91] These rituals create a space for reflection on how we honour the earth in our daily lives, how we contribute to the cycles of growth, and how we give thanks for the nourishment that sustains us. The symbolism of wheat during Lammas reminds us of the intimate relationship between humanity and the natural world, and the sacredness of the earth's cycles in both physical and spiritual terms.

In Action

The exercises in this section invite you to explore and experience the processes of growth and harvest and rewards for effort or investment. By participating in these activities, you will encounter aspects of the nature of the Wheat rune to assist in deepening your understanding of this symbol.

Plant Seeds

Grow something from seed, preferably something you can harvest and consume. Investigate what grows well in your area and select for preference (taste) and suitability to your living situation. Once you have selected your crop, your objective

91. Winter, *Witchcraft Discovered*, 78–79.

is to tend it to the point of harvest and consumption. Pay attention to the experience at the varying stages, the difficulties you might encounter, and the joy or anticipation of the growing cycle. When you harvest and consume the plant, allow your mind to review the entire process and experience gratitude for this journey you shared with the plant. Think about how this impacts your perspectives of food or the pleasure of eating it.

Make Bread

Find a simple bread recipe and try making your own loaf. You can offer part of this to the land where you live in a simple ritual of gratitude but also bring your awareness to the process of eating. Reflect on the destruction of this thing you have created and the consequent benefits of this process (sustenance).

Create a Harvest Talisman

In the explorations of myth and folklore earlier in the chapter, we touched on the practice of weaving wheat or other grains into charms for protection and prosperity. Try making a simple corn dolly, a woven wheat charm, or a small bundle of dried grains to hang in your home or place on your altar. As you craft it, focus on the themes of fertility, abundance, and protection.

Make Your Own Wheat Stone

Before choosing a stone for this rune, take some time to reflect on what wheat symbolises to you. Consider its role in mythology, seasonal festivals such as Lammas, and your own experiences with harvest—whether literal or symbolic. You may also find it helpful to revisit earlier exercises in this chapter to deepen your understanding of the rune's meaning.

When you feel ready, begin looking for a stone that feels aligned with this rune's energy. It should be a comfortable size to hold, in harmony with the rest of your rune set, and something you feel drawn to. If you're uncertain, trust your intuition and remain open to signs as you search. Some people prefer stones with a golden hue to reflect the colour of ripened wheat, while others choose smooth, natural shapes that feel organic, like grains scattered across the earth.

Once you have found the right stone, spend some time with it before marking the rune. Carry it with you for several days, hold it during meditation, or place it on your altar to attune it to your energy. If the connection doesn't feel right, don't hesitate to return the stone to nature with gratitude and continue your search.

When you are ready to inscribe the Wheat rune, choose a method that feels meaningful to you. As you work, focus on the rune's significance—what it represents to you and the lessons it embodies. Infuse the stone with your intentions, allowing it to become a tangible representation of your understanding of this symbol.

In Thought

These meditations will help you deepen your connection to the Wheat rune and its symbolism. Before beginning, take time to familiarise yourself with the rune's shape so you can visualise it clearly. If you haven't already, reflect on its meaning in relation to the themes of harvest, sustenance, and the cycles of life. For the second meditation, you may wish to record the script and listen back rather than trying to recall it as you go. Approach these practices with an open mind, allowing any insights to emerge naturally.

Meditation 1: Exploring the Wheat Stone

This meditation is unscripted and will assist you build a connection with the image of the rune. The objective is to notice any existing concepts or associations that this rune might hold for you. By performing this exercise, you will be able to witness those ideas bubbling to the surface. Take note of anything that comes up and remember there is no right or wrong here. Spend some time recording anything that comes up in your journal when you are done.

Get comfortable and close your eyes, taking several calming breaths. Check in with your body and relax any areas of tension. Let your breath carry away stress as your body softens and relaxes. Spend a minute or two settling into the exercise, setting your intention to explore the symbol of the Wheat.

With your eyes still closed, envision the symbol of the Wheat rune as clearly as you can, simply regarding it and remaining open to insights. Notice any thoughts, ideas, or memories that arise, as well as any body sensations.

Take note of these while keeping your attention gently focused on the Wheat symbol.

If your mind wanders, tenderly bring your focus back to the symbol. Aim to stay in this meditation for at least ten minutes.

You may wish to repeat this meditation several times as you work with the rune. You can also revisit it periodically to integrate new insights as your relationship deepens.

Meditation 2: Meeting the Spirit of the Wheat Rune

The following is a guided meditation. The objective here is to go on a journey to meet the spirit of the Wheat rune so that you can build a relationship with it. This has two secondary benefits: The first is the ability to learn directly from the rune spirit, and the second is to anchor that spirit in your rune stone. As we've said, we recommend recording this script and playing it back, perhaps with some calming music. If not, try memorising the steps and walking yourself through the meditation from memory. Be sure to leave adequate time at the marked pauses for interactions and input from beings within the meditation.

Begin by finding a comfortable position and closing your eyes. Take several deep, calming breaths, and let your body relax.

Take a deep breath in... and as you exhale, let go of any tension in your body. Allow yourself to settle into this moment, leaving behind any distractions or concerns. With each breath, feel yourself becoming more relaxed, more at ease.

Now, imagine yourself standing in a beautiful forest. The air is cool and fresh, and the sound of leaves rustling in the gentle breeze surrounds you. Sunlight filters through the canopy above, casting a soft dappled light onto the forest floor.

Take a moment to feel the soil beneath your feet. The earth is solid, grounding you. Each breath you take connects you more deeply with this peaceful place.

As you walk through the forest, you notice a large, ancient tree ahead of you. Its trunk is wide and strong, its bark thick and textured. There's something magical about this tree—it's as though it has been standing here for centuries, watching over the forest.

You feel drawn to the tree. As you get closer, you notice something remarkable: There is a doorway in the trunk of the tree. It's small and rounded, just large enough for you to step through. The door itself is made of smooth wood, with intricate carvings that seem to shimmer slightly in the sunlight.

Take a moment to observe this doorway. What does it look like? Notice the details, the carvings, the way it feels as you gently reach out and touch it.

Now, when you're ready, place your hand on the door's handle. It opens easily, inviting you to step inside. Take a deep breath, and with your next exhale, step through the doorway.

As you pass through, you enter a new space. This place is calm and safe, a sanctuary just for you. Perhaps it's a beautiful garden, a peaceful meadow, or a cosy room—whatever feels right to you. Take a moment to explore this space. Feel the peace that surrounds you. You are safe here, and everything you need is already within you.

Breathe in deeply, and let yourself relax even further. In this place, you are free from any worries or stress. Feel the calm washing over you, nurturing and restoring your mind and body.

Take some time here, in this space of peace and tranquillity. You can return to this place anytime you wish, simply by stepping through the doorway in the tree.

As you stand in your peaceful space, the air around you feels warm and comforting, carrying a sense of growth, fulfilment, and abundance. In the distance, you see a golden glow shimmering in the sunlight, drawing you toward it with a quiet sense of satisfaction. You follow the path ahead, and as you approach, you see tall stalks of wheat gently swaying in the breeze, glowing with the light of a golden harvest.

This is the Wheat rune. It appears before you as a symbol of the harvest—the culmination of effort, the rewards for physical work, and the abundance that comes from tending to the earth and your own endeavours. The wheat sways, full and ripe, ready to be gathered. Take a moment to stand before this rune, feeling the energy of completion, growth, and the rewards that come with perseverance.

The Wheat rune represents the cycle of effort and reward, of sowing and reaping, and reminds you that your hard work and dedication will bring you the fruits of your labour. It speaks of patience, perseverance, and the time it takes for things to grow.

Breathe deeply, allowing the golden energy of the Wheat rune to fill you. Feel it moving through your body, bringing a sense of fulfilment, gratitude, and accomplishment. You are now connected to the energy of the harvest, the rewards that come after a season of work and dedication.

As you stand in this golden field, you become aware of a presence nearby. This is the spirit of the Wheat rune, a guide who embodies the energy of harvest, abundance, and the rewards for physical work. The spirit approaches you with the calmness of a farmer who understands the rhythms of the earth, bringing with it the wisdom of patience, hard work, and the cycles of growth.

The spirit of the Wheat rune may appear as a figure with golden wheat woven into their clothing, a wise and nurturing presence, or simply as an energy that feels rich and abundant, like the earth at harvest time. Allow the spirit to take whatever form feels natural to you.

As the spirit draws near, you feel a deep sense of satisfaction, as though the long season of tending and growth has come to fruition. This spirit is here to help you reflect on the efforts you have made and to guide you in understanding the rewards that are now ready for you to receive.

Take a moment to connect with the spirit of the Wheat rune. Feel its energy of harvest and abundance, its deep understanding that the time of reward comes after the season of hard work. This spirit reminds you that your efforts have not been in vain and that the fruits of your labour are ready to be harvested.

The spirit now invites you to reflect on an area of your life where you have been working hard or waiting for results. Perhaps you have been nurturing a project, working toward a goal, or putting in physical or emotional labour. Take a moment to reflect on this area of your life, and when you are ready, silently or aloud, ask the spirit of the Wheat rune to show you the rewards of your efforts. Ask it to help you understand the harvest you are about to receive and how best to gather and appreciate the fruits of your work.

(Pause for reflection, allowing time to ask and connect.)

The spirit may respond with feelings of gratitude, images of completion, or a sense of fulfilment. It might show you the harvest that is ready for you or help you see how your hard work has led to this moment. Trust whatever comes to you, even if it feels subtle or slow. The Wheat rune teaches us that the rewards come in their own time and that patience and perseverance are always rewarded.

Take a moment to sit with the guidance you've received. Feel how the energy of the Wheat rune brings you a deep sense of accomplishment and gratitude for the journey you've been on, helping you to see the beauty and abundance of your harvest.

Now, the spirit offers you a final message—a gift of wisdom or insight about your work and the rewards you are about to receive. Open your heart and mind to receive this final message.

(Pause briefly.)

As your time with the spirit of the Wheat rune comes to an end, you feel a deep sense of peace and gratitude. The spirit begins to fade, like the golden light of the harvest sun setting on the horizon, but the feeling of fulfilment and abundance remains, filling the space with warmth and contentment.

Take a deep breath, knowing that you can return to this space and this spirit whenever you seek guidance or need to reflect on the fruits of your labour. The energy of the Wheat rune is always within you, reminding you of the rewards that come with perseverance and hard work.

Now, turn away from the rune and begin to walk back toward the doorway in the tree. As you move through your peaceful space, you carry the golden energy of the Wheat rune with you, knowing that its abundance and rewards will continue to unfold in your life.

Step through the doorway once again, returning to the forest. Feel the ground beneath your feet, hear the soft rustling of the leaves in the breeze, and sense the calmness of the forest as you return to the present.

With each breath, bring yourself back to the present moment. Begin to notice your body again, feeling the surface beneath you, the air on your skin.

When you are ready, gently open your eyes, feeling calm, fulfilled, and connected to the energy of the harvest.

When you have finished, take a moment to record your insights: What did you see? What have you learnt? Did anything surprise you? As part of your records, you can sketch out any particularly vivid imagery that came through your meditation as a way of grounding it into the physical world.

You might also like to try a grounding exercise to help bring you back to the present moment. This can be achieved by standing barefoot on the earth, imagining energetic roots reaching from your feet into the ground and balancing your energy, or resting your forehead on the floor for a moment.

In Words

Take some time to reflect on your experiences with the Wheat rune and record your insights in your journal. Begin by noting anything that stood out to you during the previous exercises. Did any particular symbols, feelings, or ideas emerge as you worked with this rune? Consider the themes of harvest, nourishment, and the cycles of growth and renewal. How do they manifest in your own life?

If you experimented with making bread, write down the recipe you used and reflect on the process. How did it feel to work with grain in such a tangible way? Did the act of kneading, shaping, and baking deepen your understanding of the rune? Note any observations about the final result: Was it successful? What would you change next time?

Expand your exploration by considering other plants associated with sustenance and cycles of growth. Make a list of plants you might like to cultivate, whether for food, ritual, or personal connection. What draws you to these particular plants? How do they relate to the symbolism of wheat and the harvest?

Finally, bring everything together by formulating your own interpretation of the Wheat rune. Write down what this symbol now means to you, incorporating the insights gained from research, meditation, and practical work. Has your perspective shifted since you first encountered the rune? If so, in what ways? This is your personal understanding of the Wheat rune. Let it evolve naturally as you continue your journey.

Chapter Ten
The Crossed Spears Stone

The spears on the Crossed Spears stone are usually represented by simple arrow shapes, crossed over and both pointing diagonally upwards. In some systems, such as Sheppard's Witches' Runes, there is an arrow at both ends of the spears, and the stone is referred to as the Crossroads.

We have typically seen this symbol represented in black, but some authors, such as Crowther, suggest it should be done in red paint.[92] Both stark, dramatic colours can be chosen to drive home the seriousness of the quarrels and conflicts that this stone can represent.

The symbol on the Crossed Spears stone serves as a reminder to proceed carefully or stop and wait. The stone can sometimes represent the strife between two people or the person causing the strife; sometimes it can indicate a person who is in direct opposition of the querent's plans.

In a Reading

According to Ashcroft-Nowicki and others, the Crossed Spears stone traditionally represents quarrels and war as well as suggesting a state of great danger that advises caution. This imagery serves as a stark reminder to pause and assess the situation before moving forward, as it may signal imminent conflict or discord.

92. Crowther, *Lid Off the Cauldron*, 112.

There is potential that someone is directly opposing you or your plans. Sometimes this stone can represent *both* the conflict and the person you are in conflict with. In her book *Lid off the Cauldron,* Crowther suggested that the Crossed Spears rune indicates a sudden promotion if the querent is in the armed forces.[93]

Additionally, some interpretations view the crossed spears as a crossroads, embodying a pivotal moment where multiple paths lie before you. This encourages careful consideration of the choices ahead, highlighting the importance of weighing potential outcomes before deciding on a course of action. Ultimately, the Crossed Spears rune invites reflection on both external conflicts and internal dilemmas, urging you to navigate these challenges with wisdom and foresight.

In Culture and Mythology

Spears, arrows, war, and conflict appear in myths across cultures, often symbolising power, protection, and the trials of battle—both physical and spiritual. From the legendary weapons of gods and heroes to sacred duels and cosmic struggles, these symbols reveal deeper truths about fate, honour, and the balance between destruction and defence. Whether wielded by divine warriors, enchanted to strike with unerring precision, or representing the clash of opposing forces, the imagery of crossed spears carries a rich and complex legacy. In this section, we will explore myths that illuminate the deeper meanings behind this symbol.

Protection and Defence

The act of crossing two spears creates a boundary—both literal and symbolic—signifying defence, vigilance, and the readiness to stand against threats. This imagery is often associated with warriors, guardians, and sacred spaces, where the placement of crossed weapons marks an area as protected or warns outsiders to proceed with caution. The act of crossing spears creates a threshold, making it clear that beyond this point, entry is either forbidden or must be earned through challenge or negotiation.

In some cultures, crossed spears were displayed at the entrances of villages or sacred sites to deter invaders or malevolent spirits. In parts of Africa, for example, warrior societies used crossed weapons as a sign that a settlement was under protection, both by its warriors and the spiritual forces they invoked. In ancient

93. Crowther, *Lid Off the Cauldron,* 112.

Rome, a symbolic act of crossing spears was used to create a temporary boundary during military negotiations, marking a neutral ground where discussions could take place under the gods' watchful eyes.[94] Norse mythology also reflects this idea. Odin's spear, Gungnir, never misses its mark, and the crossing of spears in battle could be seen as a form of divine intervention, marking a space where fate itself would decide the victor.[95] Even in medieval Europe, crossed swords or spears above a doorway could serve as a talisman against harm, reinforcing the belief that weapons, when properly placed, could serve as both a physical and a magical defence.[96]

Alliances

In ancient warfare, spears were a prevalent weapon due to their versatility and effectiveness, particularly in close combat or during massed formations. The art of crossing spears held significant meaning beyond its literal use as a defensive tactic. In some situations, the crossing of spears symbolised the unification of warriors, often marking the moment when two or more groups came together to face a common enemy. This act was not just a gesture of physical alignment but also a symbolic one, representing the solidarity and cooperation of those fighting side by side. By crossing their spears, warriors signified that their individual purposes were now united, bound by a shared mission or goal.

Crossed spears could symbolise alliances between tribes, armies, or nations. A notable example of this can be found in the history of the Maori people of New Zealand. When different *iwi* (tribes) came together in times of war or to create peace, the crossing of spears or other weapons was a ceremonial act that formalised the alliance. This practice was not limited to combat; it also carried over into rituals and negotiations, marking the moment when two sides would agree to support each other in battle or in matters of governance.[97] By crossing their weapons, they symbolised trust, mutual respect, and a shared commitment to a common cause. The act of crossing spears, therefore, held a deep cultural significance, not only as

94. Nótári, "The Spear as the Symbol of Property and Power in Ancient Rome," 231–57.
95. Sturluson, *Edda*.
96. "Swords, Crossed."
97. Evans, *Māori Weapons in Pre-European New Zealand*, 18, 35–36.

a mark of military readiness but as a symbol of the strength that comes from unity and alliance in the face of adversity.

Conflict

In contrast, crossed spears also symbolise conflict or confrontation. This concept is beautifully encapsulated by the Five of Wands tarot card, which depicts five individuals holding wands, each engaged in a struggle or competition. The imagery often shows the figures in dynamic, active postures, with their wands raised and crossed in an apparent conflict. The background may feature chaotic or tumultuous energy, symbolising the discord that arises when multiple forces, ideas, or people clash. The scene conveys a sense of challenge, struggle, and competition.

The Five of Wands typically represents conflict, but not necessarily in the form of violence or aggression. It often points to a situation where there is a disagreement, rivalry, or differing opinions leading to friction. This conflict can be external, such as competition at work or a heated discussion with others, or internal, where you may feel torn between competing goals or desires.[98]

The Five of Wands typically urges people to engage with challenges and confront the sources of tension in their life, suggesting that these struggles can lead to growth and development if approached constructively. Conversely, the Crossed Spears rune tends to serve as a warning about conflict. Looking at it from the perspective of the tarot, we see an interesting nuance to the appearance of conflict in a reading. Instead of retreating from conflict, the card may encourage you to find ways to navigate it effectively, learning from different perspectives while remaining true to your own values. It emphasises that conflict, when managed with understanding, can ultimately lead to collaboration, new ideas, and progress.

Sacred and Ritual Power

Spears have ritual significance in many mythologies, often connected to deities of war, hunting, or the earth. The crossing of spears can be a ritualistic act, symbolising an offering or a sacred bond with the gods, particularly in warrior cultures. In Norse mythology, spears are associated with Odin, and crossed spears might represent his protection or divine judgment.[99]

---

98. Waite, *The Pictorial Key to the Tarot*, 188–89.
99. Sturluson, *Edda*.

The Way Is Barred

The image of two guards standing at a doorway armed with spears has become common in popular imagination. At the approach of an unwelcome guest, the weapons would be lowered, effectively barring entry. In folklore across Europe, many superstitions exist around the placing of a cross above or near a door to prevent evil from passing through.[100] This notion overlaps with the idea of protection and defence, but it is seen from the other side of the metaphoric door. In this light, we see that protections can work for or against us and, in the latter context, would represent an obstacle or dead end in our journey.

Crossroads

An alternate perspective on this symbol is that it represents two paths crossing, or a literal crossroads. In this way we can see the idea of collision or otherwise indecision or change. In folklore, the crossroads are often seen as a place of great spiritual and supernatural significance, symbolising a point of transition, choice, and connection between worlds. They are frequently believed to be a meeting point for deities, spirits, and otherworldly forces, where one can summon or encounter supernatural beings. In many traditions, including African and European folklore, the crossroads are linked to magic, divination, and pacts with spirits or the devil.[101] For instance, the famous legend of the blues musician Robert Johnson tells of him selling his soul to the devil at a crossroads in exchange for musical talent.[102] Crossroads represent both opportunities and dangers, offering the potential for transformation or misfortune.

In Action

By reflecting on these activities, you can deepen your connection to the symbolism of the Crossed Spears. Conflict, protection, boundaries, and crossroads all represent powerful themes in the journey of life, and by exploring them through your own experiences, you gain insights that tie into the rune's meaning in a personal way.

---

100. Opie and Tatem, *A Dictionary of Superstitions*, 108–9.
101. Drury, *The Watkins Dictionary of Magic*, 64.
102. Taylor, "The Devil and the Crossroads."

Reflect on Conflict

Think of a time in your life when you were actively opposed by someone or your actions were hindered in some way. This could be a situation where you felt blocked, challenged, or unable to move forward. As you reflect on this, focus on the emotions and physical sensations that arise. How did it feel in your body during the experience? Did your chest tighten, stomach knot, or posture change? Try to relive the experience as vividly as possible and allow your mind to wander through the emotions and thoughts you had at the time.

After you've revisited the experience, reflect on how it was resolved. Did the conflict end through an agreement, a fight, or a shift in perspective? How did your feelings about the situation change over time? Was there a form of reconciliation, or was it left unresolved? Journaling about this experience will help you connect your personal understanding of opposition and how crossed spears, as a symbol of defence and conflict, might relate to your life.

Sensations of Guarded Spaces

Consider a moment when you encountered a physical or metaphorical guard. This could be anything from a security officer at a building entrance to encountering a literal or figurative boundary—such as being stopped at a checkpoint or facing a situation where access was restricted. How did you feel when you encountered these guarded spaces? Did you feel a sense of protection, unease, or even a desire to push against the limit?

Reflect on the emotions and body sensations that arose during the experience. Did it create a sense of safety, or did it evoke frustration or anxiety? Write down your thoughts on the purpose of the guard—were they keeping you safe, or were they an obstacle? What do these sensations suggest about your relationship to boundaries, protection, or defence?

Make a Protective Ritual or Charm

Use the Crossed Spears as a motif in a protection charm, amulet, or ritual. You might create an object with the rune symbolised by crossed objects, such as two twigs or sticks, or even a drawing of the rune itself. Create a small ritual around this item, such as placing it near your doorway or keeping it in a sacred space to invoke protection and ward off negative influences.

As you create your charm, consider the significance of protection in your life. Whom or what are you seeking to protect? How does the act of crafting this protective item help you channel the energy of the Crossed Spears?

Stand at a Crossroads

Take some time to find a crossroads—this could be a literal intersection of paths in nature, a street corner, or even just a point in your life where you feel faced with multiple choices. Stand in the centre of this crossroads, and as you do, focus on the feeling of being at the meeting point of many possibilities. Let your body relax and be present in this moment. What impressions arise as you consider this place of multiple options?

From this position, let your mind roam. What thoughts come to you when you consider the weight of possibility and the choices that lie before you? How do you feel when imagining the crossroads as a symbol of potential—the many ways you could go, the directions you could take? Take time to journal your experience. Did you feel excitement, fear, indecision, or clarity? This activity helps tap into the symbolism of the crossed spears, as it represents the coming together of forces and options, much like how opposing entities or choices intersect at a pivotal point.

Make Your Own Crossed Spears Stone

To make your own Crossed Spears rune, begin by selecting a stone that feels right for the symbol. As with the other runes, choose something that resonates with you. The material should feel sturdy, as it will symbolise the strength and protection that the Crossed Spears represent. The physical weight of the material can also help ground you in the intention of defence, structure, and the potential tension between opposing forces.

Take time to connect with your stone, holding it in your hands and focusing on its texture, weight, and feel. Let it become familiar to you, setting your intention for the creation process.

To carve or inscribe the rune, use a method that feels appropriate for your chosen material. As you inscribe the Crossed Spears, focus on the symbolism: the intersection between two opposing forces, the protective barrier they form, and the resilience that is created from their union. Take your time as you carve or draw the rune. Let the process be meditative, allowing the act of creation to deepen your connection to the meaning of the Crossed Spears.

Finally, as you hold your completed Crossed Spears rune, take a moment to reflect on its meaning. Keep the stone in a place where you can see it regularly, or carry it with you to remind yourself of the strength that comes from balancing opposing forces in your life.

In Thought

Before starting the following two meditations, take some time to get familiar with the Crossed Spears symbol. You are ready to proceed once you can clearly visualise the rune with your eyes closed. For the second meditation, you might like to record yourself reading the script and then listen back so that you can be fully immersed in the experience.

Meditation 1: Exploring the Crossed Spears Stone

The following meditation is unscripted and will help you build a connection with the image of the rune. The objective is to notice any existing concepts or associations that this rune might hold for you. By performing this exercise, you will be able to witness those ideas bubbling to the surface. Take note of anything that comes up and remember there is no right or wrong here. Spend some time recording anything that comes up in your journal when you are done.

Get comfortable and close your eyes, taking several calming breaths. Check in with your body, relaxing any tension you feel. Let your breath carry away stress as you soften and relax. Spend a minute here to settle in and set the intention to explore the symbol of the Crossed Spears.

With your eyes still closed, visualise the symbol clearly in your mind. Simply regard it and remain open to insights. Notice any thoughts, ideas, or body sensations that arise, and take note of them while keeping your focus on the Crossed Spears.

If your attention wanders, gently return to the symbol. Aim to stay in this meditation for at least ten minutes.

You may wish to repeat it several times as you work with this rune. You can also revisit it periodically to integrate new insights.

Meditation 2: Meeting the Spirit of the Crossed Spears Rune

This is the more in-depth meditation. The objective here is to go on a journey to meet the spirit of the Crossed Spears rune so that you can build a relationship with it. This has two secondary benefits: The first is the ability to learn directly from the rune spirit, and the second is to anchor that spirit in your rune stone. Record this script, if you wish, so you can play it back, possibly with some calming music, or otherwise memorise the steps and walk yourself through the meditation. Be sure to leave adequate time at the marked pauses for interactions and input from beings within the meditation.

Begin by finding a comfortable position and closing your eyes. Take several deep, calming breaths, and let your body relax.

Take a deep breath in ... and as you exhale, let go of any tension in your body. Allow yourself to settle into this moment, leaving behind any distractions or concerns. With each breath, feel yourself becoming more relaxed, more at ease.

Now, imagine yourself standing in a beautiful forest. The air is cool and fresh, and the sound of leaves rustling in the gentle breeze surrounds you. Sunlight filters through the canopy above, casting a soft dappled light onto the forest floor.

Take a moment to feel the soil beneath your feet. The earth is solid, grounding you. Each breath you take connects you more deeply with this peaceful place.

As you walk through the forest, you notice a large, ancient tree ahead of you. Its trunk is wide and strong, its bark thick and textured. There's something magical about this tree—it's as though it has been standing here for centuries, watching over the forest.

You feel drawn to the tree. As you get closer, you notice something remarkable: There is a doorway in the trunk of the tree. It's small and rounded, just large enough for you to step through. The door itself is made of smooth wood, with intricate carvings that seem to shimmer slightly in the sunlight.

Take a moment to observe this doorway. What does it look like? Notice the details, the carvings, the way it feels as you gently reach out and touch it.

Now, when you're ready, place your hand on the door's handle. It opens easily, inviting you to step inside. Take a deep breath, and with your next exhale, step through the doorway.

As you pass through, you enter a new space. This place is calm and safe, a sanctuary just for you. Perhaps it's a beautiful garden, a peaceful meadow, or a cosy room—whatever feels right to you. Take a moment to explore this space. Feel the peace that surrounds you. You are safe here, and everything you need is already within you.

Breathe in deeply and let yourself relax even further. In this place, you are free from any worries or stress. Feel the calm washing over you, nurturing and restoring your mind and body.

Take some time here, in this space of peace and tranquillity. You can return to this place anytime you wish, simply by stepping through the doorway in the tree.

As you stand in your peaceful space, a subtle tension begins to form in the air around you. There is a stillness, like the quiet before a storm, and you feel a sense of anticipation, as if something is waiting to be revealed. In the distance, you see a faint metallic gleam. You are drawn toward it with a sense of purpose. You begin to walk, feeling both cautious and curious, and soon you arrive at the source of the gleam: two spears, crossed in front of you, their sharp points glinting in the light.

This is the Crossed Spears rune. It appears before you as a symbol of quarrels, conflict, and potential danger. The Crossed Spears represent a meeting point of tension, a moment of decision, or a sign to hold back and assess the situation before moving forward. Take a moment to stand before this rune, feeling its energy of protection and challenge, of danger and warning.

The Crossed Spears rune speaks of confrontation, not just in the outer world but also within yourself. It represents the times when you face opposition, conflict, or inner turmoil, when the path ahead is uncertain or fraught with tension. The spears remind you that some situations call for caution, patience, or a strategic pause.

Breathe deeply, allowing the energy of the Crossed Spears rune to enter your body. Feel the tension in the air around you, the sense of readiness, and the need to observe and reflect before acting. You are now connected to the energy of caution and protection, and the wisdom of waiting.

As you stand in this space, you become aware of another presence nearby. This is the spirit of the Crossed Spears rune, a guide who embodies the energy of conflict, protection, and strategic patience. The spirit approaches you with an air of strength and wisdom, holding both the power of a warrior and the insight of one who knows when to wait and when to act.

The spirit of the Crossed Spears rune may appear as a warrior figure, clad in armour, or as a presence that feels firm and protective, like a shield against danger. Allow the spirit to take whatever form feels natural to you.

As the spirit draws near, you feel a sense of caution and power. This spirit is here to help you understand the conflict or tension you may be experiencing in your life and to guide you in navigating it with wisdom. The Crossed Spears rune teaches that not every battle must be fought immediately and that sometimes the greatest strength lies in knowing when to wait and when to act.

Take a moment to connect with the spirit of the Crossed Spears rune. Feel its energy of protection and readiness. This spirit embodies the understanding that conflict is sometimes inevitable, but how you respond to it can make all the difference. It is here to show you how to assess the situation with clarity and how to protect yourself from unnecessary harm.

The spirit now invites you to reflect on an area of your life where you are facing conflict, danger, or a difficult decision. Perhaps there is tension with others, a challenging situation, or an inner struggle where you feel pulled in opposing directions. Take a moment to reflect on this area of your life, and when you are ready, silently or aloud, ask the spirit of the Crossed Spears rune for guidance. Ask it to show you whether this is a time to act or a time to wait and how best to navigate this moment of tension or conflict.

(Pause for reflection.)

The spirit may respond with a sense of stillness, urging you to wait and gather more information, or with a feeling of readiness, encouraging you to take action with confidence. It might show you a new perspective on the conflict or help you understand the danger and how to avoid it. Trust whatever comes to you, even if it feels subtle or uncertain. The Crossed Spears rune teaches us that danger often lies not only in the situation itself but in how we choose to respond to it.

Take a moment to sit with the guidance you've received. Feel how the energy of the Crossed Spears rune brings you clarity about the situation, helping you to make wise and measured decisions, whether that means holding back for now or stepping forward with purpose.

Now, the spirit offers you a final message—a gift of insight or strength as you face the conflict or challenge in your life. Open your heart and mind to receive this final message.

(Pause to receive the message.)

As your time with the spirit of the Crossed Spears rune comes to an end, you feel a deep sense of gratitude and calm. The spirit begins to withdraw, like a warrior lowering their weapons after a battle, but the feeling of strength and readiness remains, filling the space with protection and clarity.

Take a deep breath, knowing that you can return to this space and this spirit whenever you face conflict or uncertainty in your life. The energy of the Crossed Spears rune is always within you, guiding you to make wise decisions, to protect yourself when necessary, and to know when to act and when to wait.

Now, turn away from the rune and begin to walk back toward the doorway in the tree. As you move through your peaceful space, you carry the protective energy of the Crossed Spears rune with you, knowing that its strength and wisdom will continue to guide you in times of tension or conflict.

Step through the doorway once again, returning to the forest. Feel the solid ground beneath your feet, hear the stillness of the trees around you, and sense the calmness of the forest as you return to the present.

With each breath, bring yourself back to the present moment. Begin to notice your body again, feeling the surface beneath you, the air on your skin.

When you are ready, gently open your eyes, feeling calm, clear, and connected to the energy of protection and wisdom.

When you have finished, take a moment to record your insights: What did you see? What have you learnt? Did anything surprise you? As part of your records, you can sketch out any particularly vivid imagery that came through your meditation as a way of grounding it into the physical world.

You might also like to try a grounding exercise to help bring you back to the present moment. This can be achieved by standing barefoot on the earth, imagining energetic roots reaching from your feet into the ground and balancing your energy, or resting your forehead on the floor for a moment.

In Words

Take a moment to look back at the activities you've completed so far. Record your thoughts, feelings, and insights into your journal. What stood out to you during the exercises? Did anything surprise you about your reactions or thoughts? Were there any physical sensations that you noticed, such as tension or resistance? Explore the emotions that arose and how these experiences might relate to the Crossed Spears rune.

Delve into the history and symbolism of crossed weapons or the crossroads in various mythologies, folklore, or cultural traditions. Perhaps you find stories of warriors crossing spears as a protective gesture or of crossroads as places of choice, decision, or transition. Choose one story or example that resonates with you and write it down. Reflect on how the story connects with the idea of conflict, protection, or the balance between opposing forces.

Think about the symbolism of both the crossroads and the crossed spears. Do you feel more drawn to one over the other? Why do you think that is? What do these symbols evoke in you emotionally and mentally? Write about your personal connection to both ideas and what they represent in your life.

Now that you've explored the exercises and reflected on the symbolism, it's time to define the Crossed Spears rune in your own words. What does this rune mean to you? What themes have emerged from your exploration of conflict, protection, and opposition? How do these ideas show up in your life? Do you see the need for protection or boundaries, or do you relate more to the challenge of opposing forces? Write a detailed interpretation of the rune, integrating insights from your research, experiences, and emotional reactions. Consider how this rune could serve you as a tool for understanding conflict or finding strength in times of struggle.

By writing about your experiences, research, and personal reflections, you can deepen your connection to the Crossed Spears rune and bring its lessons into your everyday life.

Chapter Eleven
The Star Stone

The Star is usually portrayed as a stylised sketch of a single shining body. Sometimes this is as simple as a sketch of what resembles a large asterisk. The simple shining imagery of the Star speaks of the wishes, hopes, ambitions, and goals of the subject of the reading. Its appearance in a reading is often an invitation to reflect on the *why* of our plans and remind ourselves of what it is that drives us forward even when those plans don't come to fruition the way we hope.

In a Reading

The Star rune carries the traditional meanings of hopes and wishes, and it is often regarded as a positive sign in divination. It symbolises the aspirations that guide us, illuminating our path toward desires and goals. When this rune appears, it invites us to reflect on what draws us forward—our dreams, our ambitions, and the callings that resonate within us. It encourages us to embrace our potential and trust in the journey ahead, reminding us that our aspirations are not just distant ideals but vibrant energies that shape our present and future.

In essence, the Star rune serves as a beacon of inspiration, urging us to pursue our passions and believe in the possibilities that lie ahead.

In Culture and Mythology

Throughout history, stars have been powerful symbols in myth and legend, representing hope, guidance, and destiny. They are lights in the darkness, offering direction to travellers and seekers alike, whether in a literal sense—guiding sailors across vast seas—or in a spiritual or mystical sense, illuminating paths to wisdom and transformation. Many cultures have linked stars to divine forces, fate, and cosmic order, seeing them as messengers of the gods or omens of great events. In this section, we will explore the myths and stories that weave stars into the fabric of human belief, revealing their lasting significance across time and tradition.

The North Star

Stars have served as beacons of guidance for countless cultures throughout history, both in a practical sense and as profound symbols of direction and purpose. The North Star (Polaris) is one of the most enduring examples, known for its fixed position in the night sky. It has been a steadfast guide for travellers, sailors, and explorers from many cultures. For example, in Norse mythology, Polaris is associated with the World Axis, Yggdrasil, the great cosmic tree that connects the heavens, earth, and Underworld. The Vikings relied on the North Star for navigation during their long sea voyages, ensuring they stayed on course.

In ancient China, Polaris was regarded as the celestial emperor's seat, a stable and unchanging centre around which the heavens revolved. It symbolised order, constancy, and rightful rule, supporting the emperor's divine mandate. Similarly, in Indigenous North American traditions, stars often played a role in guiding migrations and seasonal movements. The Lakota people, for instance, aligned their sacred sites with star patterns, believing the stars provided a cosmic blueprint for life on Earth.[103]

The Divine and Heroic

Stars have long been seen as more than mere celestial bodies, often being viewed as manifestations of divine power, the dwelling places of gods, or the final resting place of great heroes. In many traditions, stars represent the bridge between the mortal and the Divine, linking humanity to the vast and mysterious cosmos.

---

103. Johnson, "Meet Polaris, the North Star."

One of the most striking ways this symbolism appears is through the process of *catasterism*, the transformation of a mortal being—often a hero, ruler, or mythical figure—into a star or constellation. In Greek mythology, this is a common fate for those who perform extraordinary deeds or suffer tragic fates. Orion, the great hunter, was placed among the stars by Zeus after his death, forming the well-known constellation that bears his name. Similarly, Castor and Pollux, the divine twins of the Dioscuri, were given a place in the heavens as the constellation Gemini, allowing them to remain together for eternity.

The Romans also adopted this idea, particularly in their imperial cult, where deceased emperors were believed to ascend to the stars upon death. Julius Caesar was famously declared a god after his passing, and a bright comet that appeared during his funeral games was interpreted as his soul rising to join the celestial realm. This notion underscored the divine authority of Rome's rulers, linking their power to the heavens.

Destiny

Stars are frequently linked to ideas of fate or destiny. In Greco-Roman thought, the belief in astral influence gave rise to astrology, where individual fates were written in the stars. In astrology, the positions and movements of stars and planets are believed to influence human lives and events. This association ties stars to the idea of predestination and cosmic order.

The concept of following one's star to fulfil a destined path echoes in many traditions, including the biblical story of the Star of Bethlehem, which guided the Magi to the birthplace of Christ. Whether as literal waypoints or symbolic lights leading the soul toward wisdom, stars remain powerful emblems of guidance.

The Tarot

In the Rider-Waite-Smith classic tarot system, the Star card comes seventeenth in the major arcana and is a symbol of hope, inspiration, and renewal. It represents a sense of calm and optimism, often following a period of hardship or difficulty. Key meanings of the Star card include aspirations, desires, renewal, inspiration and clarity, spiritual connection, and healing.[104] Overall, it is a positive and uplifting

104. Waite, *The Pictorial Key to the Tarot*, 136–39.

card that encourages embracing optimism and following one's true path with a renewed sense of purpose and hope.

Hope

Stars are seen as symbols of hope and light in the darkness, offering guidance when the path ahead is uncertain. They represent inspiration, dreams, and aspirations, encouraging people to reach beyond their current circumstances toward something greater. The sight of a clear starry sky can evoke wonder and a sense of limitless possibility, stirring the imagination and the pursuit of higher ideals. Frequently they appear as beacons of protection, fortune, and divine presence, reminding us that even in the darkest times, light still shines above. This sentiment is captured by the light of Eärendil, which is given to Frodo by Galadriel during his quest in *The Lord of the Rings.*

Wishing Upon a Star

It is a common idea to wish on stars, often falling stars or the first star you see of a night. This belief points to an integral aspect of the idea around stars being connected to our wishes. In Disney's *Pinocchio,* the catalyst for the story is a wish made on a star. The practice of wishing on stars speaks to our cultural history of viewing them as beings with the power to influence our lives and destiny, whether through astrology or their relationship to heroes and divine powers.

Wisdom

The stars, as part of the heavens, were often viewed as sources of great knowledge, holding the secrets of fate, time, and cosmic order. In many ancient societies, astronomy and astrology were deeply intertwined with wisdom, guiding everything from agriculture to governance. Civilisations such as Babylonians, Egyptians, Chinese, and Maya all placed great importance on celestial movements, believing that the stars revealed divine will and the rhythms of existence. Babylonian priests developed some of the earliest astrological systems, using the positions of planets and stars to predict events on earth. In ancient Egypt, the heliacal rising of Sirius marked the flooding of the Nile, a crucial event for agriculture. Similarly, in China, astrology was tied to the imperial court, with celestial omens influencing decisions of rulers.[105] Across cultures, the careful study of the stars was seen as a way to unlock hidden truths, offering insights into natural phenomena, human destiny, and the unfolding of time itself.

Campfires of the Ancestors

The stars are seen as connected with the dead in various ways by different cultures across time. We have already mentioned the memorialisation of heroes or important figures in stars and constellations. Aboriginal Australian peoples have their own lore and stories about the stars. The Yolngu people, first nations peoples of north-east Arnhem Land in Australia, recognise the stars as the campfires of their ancestors. The dimmer stars belong to those who began their afterlife journey a long time ago and have moved farther away, while the brighter stars belong to the more recently deceased.[106]

In Action

The following activities will help you to identify, engage with, and explore the stars and your relationship to them. By building out personal experiences with the stars, you will develop and deepen your understanding of their symbolism and how they relate to you.

Observe the Night Sky

On a clear night, go outside and spend some time simply looking up at the stars. You might need to get out of the city to do this if you live in an area with particularly bad light pollution. Take in the vastness of the sky and allow yourself to be present with it. What emotions or thoughts arise as you gaze at the stars? Do you feel a sense of awe, insignificance, connection, or curiosity? Write down any sensations, images, or insights that come to you.

Track the Stars Over Time

If you are familiar with any constellations or bright stars, try to locate them in the sky. If not, look for patterns that stand out to you. Return to the same spot on different nights over the course of a week or one to several months and observe

105. Drury, *The Watkins Dictionary of the Esoteric*, 21–22.
106. "The Stars."

how the stars shift their position. What does this movement suggest to you? How might this shifting landscape have influenced the myths and stories people told about the stars? Consider how different constellations dominate the sky in different seasons and what symbolic meanings might be associated with them at different points in the year.

Use a Star-Gazing App

Download a free star-gazing app on your phone and use it to identify the stars, planets, and constellations above you. Pick at least one celestial body that catches your interest and research the lore associated with it. What myths, deities, or historical meanings are connected to it? How do these stories shape the way people have understood the night sky? Reflect on whether the myths resonate with you.

Research Local Star Lore

Investigate whether there are any specific star myths or traditions linked to the land where you live. Many Indigenous cultures have their own rich interpretations of the night sky that differ from the Greco-Roman constellations commonly known in the West. If possible, look into the star stories indigenous to your area. How do these traditions relate to the land, seasons, and cultural values? Consider journaling about how these local stories influence your understanding of the stars.

Make Your Own Star Stone

Spend some time reflecting on your connection to and understanding of the Star stone. Consider its connection to hope, wishes, and destiny. Keep these concepts in mind as you search for and fashion your own Star stone.

When selecting a stone, look for something that resonates with its themes. You might decide on something light in colour with a glossy finish or possibly something crystalline. Let your intuition guide you, but remember that your full set of runes should fit comfortably in your hand.

Once you have your stone, carry it with you for at least a week to build a connection. Take note of how it feels and whether it aligns with your ideas about the Star rune. If, after this time, the stone doesn't seem right, return it to its original place with gratitude and continue your search.

When you're ready to mark the rune, follow the instructions for your chosen method. Treat this as an intentional process, holding in mind the meaning of the Star rune and its themes of hope and inspiration.

Your finished Star rune can serve as a tool for meditation, a point of focus in your practice, or part of your divination work. As you progress through the exercises in this chapter, keep it nearby to strengthen your connection to the rune's themes of illumination, destiny, and hope.

In Thought

Before commencing the meditations in this section, take some time to familiarise yourself with the Star rune symbol earlier in this chapter. When you can confidently visualise the symbol with your eyes closed, then you can proceed to the first meditation. You might want to record yourself reading the script for the second meditation so that you can listen back to it rather than memorising the whole thing. Remember to approach both of these meditations with an open mind and take note of what comes up for you.

Meditation 1: Exploring the Star Stone

The following meditation is unscripted and will help you build a connection with the image of the Star rune. The objective is to notice any existing concepts or associations that this rune might hold for you. By performing this exercise, you will be able to witness those ideas bubbling to the surface. Take note of anything that comes up and remember there is no right or wrong here. Spend some time recording anything that comes up in your journal when you are done.

Take a moment to relax and get into a meditative state. With your eyes closed, see the symbol of the Star. See it as clearly as you can, holding it in your imagination. You do not have to do anything else; simply regard the symbol and be open to insights. Take note of anything that comes up for you during this time. What thoughts, ideas, or memories bubble up? Are there particular ideas that come to you? Body sensations? Take note of these things while letting your attention remain gently resting on the symbol of the Star.

Try to remain in this meditation for at least ten minutes.

You might like to perform this meditation several times as you work with this rune. You can also revisit it periodically to integrate new insights as your relationship grows.

Meditation 2: Meeting the Spirit of the Star Rune

This is the longer meditation that we mentioned earlier. As we noted, you might like to record this script and play it back, perhaps with some calming music, or otherwise memorise the steps and walk yourself through it. Be sure to leave adequate time at the marked pauses for interactions and input from beings within the meditation.

The objective here is to go on a journey to meet the spirit of the Star rune so that you can build a relationship with it. This has two secondary benefits: The first is the ability to learn directly from the rune spirit, and the second is to anchor that spirit in your rune stone.

Begin by finding a comfortable position and closing your eyes. Take several deep, calming breaths, and let your body relax.

Take a deep breath in... and as you exhale, let go of any tension in your body. Allow yourself to settle into this moment, leaving behind any distractions or concerns. With each breath, feel yourself becoming more relaxed, more at ease.

Now, imagine yourself standing in a beautiful forest. The air is cool and fresh, and the sound of leaves rustling in the gentle breeze surrounds you. Sunlight filters through the canopy above, casting a soft dappled light onto the forest floor.

Take a moment to feel the soil beneath your feet. The earth is solid, grounding you. Each breath you take connects you more deeply with this peaceful place.

As you walk through the forest, you notice a large, ancient tree ahead of you. Its trunk is wide and strong, its bark thick and textured. There's something magical about this tree—it's as though it has been standing here for centuries, watching over the forest.

You feel drawn to the tree. As you get closer, you notice something remarkable: There is a doorway in the trunk of the tree. It's small and rounded, just

large enough for you to step through. The door itself is made of smooth wood, with intricate carvings that seem to shimmer slightly in the sunlight.

Take a moment to observe this doorway. What does it look like? Notice the details, the carvings, the way it feels as you gently reach out and touch it.

Now, when you're ready, place your hand on the door's handle. It opens easily, inviting you to step inside. Take a deep breath, and with your next exhale, step through the doorway.

As you pass through, you enter a new space. This place is calm and safe, a sanctuary just for you. Perhaps it's a beautiful garden, a peaceful meadow, or a cosy room—whatever feels right to you. Take a moment to explore this space. Feel the peace that surrounds you. You are safe here, and everything you need is already within you.

Breathe in deeply, and let yourself relax even further. In this place, you are free from any worries or stress. Feel the calm washing over you, nurturing and restoring your mind and body.

Take some time here, in this space of peace and tranquillity. You can return to this place anytime you wish, simply by stepping through the doorway in the tree.

As you stand in your peaceful space, the air around you begins to shimmer with a soft, ethereal light. The sky above seems to grow darker, deepening into a velvety twilight, and as the darkness settles, you notice a single bright star twinkling overhead. Its light shines down on you, filling you with a sense of wonder and possibility. This gentle star calls to you, inviting you to follow its glow.

You begin to walk, following the starlight, and soon you find yourself in an open, serene space beneath a vast sky full of stars. Each one twinkles with a sense of hope and dreams, lighting up the darkness with their distant glow. In the centre of this celestial field, you see a larger, brighter star—radiating with warmth and brilliance.

This is the Star rune. It appears before you, glowing with the energy of hopes and wishes, the embodiment of dreams yet to be fulfilled. The star's light represents the aspirations that guide you, the desires that fill your heart, and the hopes that lift your spirit. Take a moment to stand before this rune, feeling the connection between your inner wishes and the vast possibilities of the universe.

The Star rune reminds you that your hopes are like stars in the night sky—always present, even when unseen, and guiding you through the darkest moments. It speaks of inspiration, dreams, and the power of wishing for a better future.

Breathe deeply, allowing the light of the Star rune to fill you. Feel it moving through your body, bringing with it a sense of possibility, faith, and wonder. You are now connected to the energy of hopes, dreams, and wishes, aligning with the star that guides you forward.

As you stand in this celestial space, you become aware of another presence nearby. This is the spirit of the Star rune, a guide who embodies the energy of dreams, hopes, and the power of wishing. The spirit approaches you with a soft, radiant glow, a presence filled with warmth and inspiration, carrying with it the magic of the stars.

The spirit of the Star rune may appear as a figure bathed in starlight, a being whose form seems to shimmer and shift like the night sky, or as an energy that feels light and uplifting, like a whisper of hope in the darkness. Allow the spirit to come to you in whatever form feels natural.

As the spirit draws near, you feel a sense of wonder and possibility. This spirit is here to guide you in connecting with your deepest hopes and wishes, helping you to understand your dreams and how they can shape your future.

Take a moment to connect with the spirit of the Star rune. Feel its energy of hope, possibility, and light. This spirit embodies the understanding that even the smallest wish can shine brightly and that your dreams are powerful forces guiding you toward your true path.

The spirit now invites you to reflect on a hope or wish you carry within you. It may be something you've longed for, a dream you've nurtured, or a desire for the future that fills your heart. Take a moment to reflect on this wish, and when you are ready, silently or aloud, ask the spirit of the Star rune to show you how to nurture this hope and how to align yourself with the energy of your deepest wishes.

(Pause.)

The spirit may respond with feelings of inspiration, images of your dreams coming to life, or a sense of knowing how to move forward with hope. It might show you the path that leads to the fulfilment of your wishes or help you understand how to remain aligned with your dreams even in challenging times. Trust whatever comes to you, even if it feels subtle or gentle. The Star rune teaches us that our hopes and dreams are like stars, guiding us through the darkest nights and reminding us that possibilities always exist.

Take a moment to sit with the guidance you've received. Feel how the energy of the Star rune fills you with hope, helping you to believe in the power of your dreams and the magic of wishing for something greater.

Now, the spirit offers you a final message—a gift of hope or inspiration as you continue on your journey toward your dreams. Open your heart and mind to receive this final message.

(Pause.)

As your time with the spirit of the Star rune comes to an end, you feel a deep sense of peace and optimism. The spirit begins to fade, like starlight at dawn, but the feeling of hope and possibility remains, filling the space with warmth and light.

Take a deep breath, knowing that you can return to this space and this spirit whenever you need to reconnect with your hopes and dreams. The energy of the Star rune is always within you, guiding you like a star in the night sky, reminding you that your wishes are powerful forces shaping your life.

Now, turn away from the rune and begin to walk back toward the doorway in the tree. As you move through your peaceful space, you carry the light of the Star rune with you, knowing that its energy will continue to inspire you and guide you toward your dreams.

Step through the doorway once again, returning to the forest. Feel the ground beneath your feet, hear the soft rustling of the leaves in the wind, and sense the peaceful energy of the forest as you return to the present.

With each breath, bring yourself back to the present moment. Begin to notice your body again, feeling the surface beneath you, the air on your skin.

When you are ready, gently open your eyes, feeling calm, inspired, and connected to the energy of your hopes and wishes.

When you have finished, take a moment to record your insights: What did you see? What have you learnt? Did anything surprise you? You can sketch out any particularly vivid imagery that came through your meditation as a way of grounding it into the physical world.

You might also like to try a grounding exercise to help bring you back to the present moment. This can be achieved by standing barefoot on the earth, imagining energetic roots reaching from your feet into the ground and balancing your energy, or resting your forehead on the floor for a moment.

In Words

After going through the exercises in this chapter, consider your thoughts on destiny, true will, or the idea of a life purpose. Do you believe in fate, or do you see life as shaped entirely by choice and circumstance? How does the concept of being guided by the stars resonate with you? Explore your relationship with desire—what does it mean to want something deeply? Do you experience desire as a force pulling you forward, or do you find it to be fleeting and changeable? Write about how you understand the state of longing, being drawn toward something, or feeling called in a particular direction.

Spend some time reflecting on the symbolism of stars in your own life. How have stars appeared in stories or personal experiences that are meaningful to you? Do they represent hope, guidance, mystery, or something else entirely? After this reflection, try writing your own interpretation of the Star rune. What does it mean to you after working through these exercises? How do the ideas of light in darkness, navigation, or celestial influence shape your understanding of this rune?

Finally, record any impressions, observations, or experiences that stood out to you during the previous activities. Whether it was a moment of insight, an unexpected emotion, or a new way of looking at the stars, capture these reflections in your journal. This will help deepen your connection to the rune and provide a record of your journey exploring its meaning.

Chapter Twelve
The Sickle Stone

The sickle or scythe is usually portrayed as a crescent-shaped blade on a short handle, sometimes with a small cross guard. Where the Wheat rune represents the rewards of the harvest, the Sickle serves as a reminder of the reaper's role in the cycle of life. Some people like to use a stone with a sharp edge for the Sickle, creating a physicality to the symbolism. This is not necessary or common.

The Sickle stone speaks of endings, cuttings-down, and death. Our reaction when we see it is often to think of grief, loss, and loneliness, but the Sickle stone reminds us of so much more. Everything that lives eventually dies, and even at an inner level, there are mindsets, values, beliefs, and behaviours that need to end to make way for newer, healthier ones. Just as we would prune a rosebush to encourage more beautiful flowers, so too should we cut back that which is no longer needed to make room for new growth.

In a Reading

The Sickle rune embodies the concept of cutting off or cutting down. It highlights the inevitability of change and the necessity of letting go, urging us to confront what must be released in order to make space for new growth. This rune can invoke feelings of loss or transformation, but it also offers a perspective on the importance of endings as part of a greater cycle. By acknowledging the reaper's presence, we learn to accept the natural rhythms of life, embracing the profound wisdom that comes from both loss and renewal.

In Culture and Mythology

The sickle holds powerful symbolism in myth and folklore, often connected to agriculture, death, and the cycle of life. As a tool used for harvesting, it represents the reaping of what has been sown, linking it to both abundance and endings. Popular depictions of figures such as the Grim Reaper or harvest deities governing the turning of the seasons have led to associations between the sickle and ideas of death and transformation. In exploring the myths surrounding the sickle, we uncover its deeper meanings—of necessary endings, renewal, and the balance between destruction and creation.

Harvest

The sickle, as a tool for harvesting crops, is strongly associated with agriculture and fertility. It symbolises abundance and the cyclical nature of life, marking the time of reaping what has been sown. In many agrarian societies, the sickle was a sacred tool tied to the earth's bounty, representing the sustenance and life force provided by the land.

Death

In some cultures, the sickle is closely linked to death, often depicted as the tool of the Grim Reaper, who uses it to "harvest" souls. The image of Death wielding a sickle or scythe conveys the inevitability of mortality and the idea that life, like crops, has a time to be harvested. This connection emphasises the cycle of life, death, and rebirth. This imagery has also carried into the cult of Santa Muerte, Saint Death, which has gained widespread popularity in Latin American countries. Unlike the Grim Reaper, Santa Muerte can be viewed as a caring figure who ensures her followers a safe passage to the afterlife.[107]

Cronos

In some mythological traditions, the sickle has divine or cosmic significance. In Greek mythology, the Titan Cronus (Saturn) used a sickle to castrate his father,

---

107. Lorentzen, "Santa Muerte."

Uranus, symbolising both the severing of power and the creation of a new order.[108] This act of cosmic rebellion represents the power of transformation and the role of the sickle in shaping the universe.

The association with Cronos also introduces the notion of time—the Titan is sometimes referred to as "Grandfather Time." The myth of Cronos eating his own children is a visceral depiction of the way time gives us new things and also consumes all things. After his own banishment by the Olympian gods, Cronos is said to watch the world from a distance, swaying his scythe like the ticking of a clock.[109] This potent image carries the message that time will always catch up to us, even if we aren't governed by him. In this way, we also see a blending of the death symbolism.

Rebellion

The sickle is sometimes associated with rebellion, often symbolising the power of the common people. Its connection to labour and the working class was amplified in modern times by its use as a symbol of revolution, particularly in the Soviet Union, where the sickle represented the peasants and their role in building a new society.[110] This reflects the tool's long-standing connection to both sustenance and struggle.

The Sickle Moon

The crescent shape of the sickle links it to lunar symbolism, particularly in relation to goddesses of the moon and the feminine Divine. In some traditions, the sickle's curved form echoes the phases of the moon, symbolising cycles of growth, fertility, and mystery. Lunar deities, such as Hecate or Selene from the Greek pantheon, are sometimes depicted with sickles, emphasising their control over the natural world and life cycles. This also reflects the connection between agriculture and the phases of the moon.

108. Fry, *Mythos*, 27–28.
109. Fry, *Mythos*, 68–69.
110. Bird, "Why Did the Soviet Union Adopt the Hammer and Sickle, and How Did It Become a Symbol of Communist Revolution?"

The Ankou

In Breton folklore, the Ankou is a death figure similar to the Grim Reaper, often portrayed as a skeletal figure holding a sickle or scythe. The Ankou is seen as the personification of death, coming to take souls from the world.[111] In this tradition, the sickle is a clear marker of death and the end of life's cycle while also emphasising the respect for this natural transition.

In Action

Exploring the significance of the Sickle rune can involve both practical and reflective activities, helping to connect the symbolic and metaphysical aspects of the rune to personal experience. The following exercises are designed to help deepen your understanding and insight.

Harvest

In honour of the agricultural aspect of the sickle, you might choose to harvest something—whether it's a garden crop or a wild plant that's in season. As you cut or gather, consider the cyclical nature of growth, death, and renewal. Reflect on how harvesting represents the culmination of a cycle and how you can use this symbolism to understand endings in your own life.

Perform a Cleansing Ritual with the Sickle Rune

Consider using the Sickle rune in a ritual of release or transformation. This could involve writing down things you wish to let go of—whether they are negative habits, relationships, or old emotions—and then symbolically "cutting them away" using the Sickle symbol. You can do this in the form of a ceremonial burning or burying of the written words or even through creating a piece of artwork where you slice through the old to make space for new growth. A classic example of this sort of work would be cutting a cord to represent severing bonds.

Walk at Dusk

Since the Sickle also symbolises the harvest and death, it's a great opportunity to go for a mindful walk at dusk or dawn—times of transition. As you walk,

---

111. "Ankou," *Oxford Reference*, accessed March 2025, https://www.oxfordreference.com/view/10.1093/oi/authority.20110803095414434.

consider the transformation of day into night, the end of one cycle and the beginning of the next. This activity can help you tune into the rhythm of life and death as it plays out in the natural world, offering insights into how these cycles manifest in your life.

Honour the Dead

Do some research to locate the graves of your ancestors or deceased relatives. Organise a trip to tend to their graves, cleaning the space and leaving some offerings of flowers or candles. Spend time contemplating the generations that made way for your life and honour them while keeping sight of the fact that life is transient.

If you do not know your ancestors or family and are unable to perform this activity, you might like to visit the graves of important people related to your field or the place you live or grew up. Ancestors can be more than just our blood relatives.

Make Your Own Sickle Stone

Before crafting your Sickle stone, take time to reflect on the meaning of this symbol. The Sickle rune carries messages of endings, severance, and transitions. Think about moments of finality or transformation between phases of your life. Bring all of this to the stone as you prepare it.

When choosing a stone for this rune, you might like something that has qualities of a blade or a jagged edge like something torn away. Let your intuition guide you but remember that your full set of runes should be comfortable to use and hold with cupped hands. If you need guidance, refer to the "Selecting Your Stones" section in chapter 2.

Once you have your stone, spend some time with it to build a connection and ensure it is the right choice. About a week is a good time frame to carry it with you. If you decide it is not the right stone, return it to where you found it with gratitude and resume your search.

When you're ready to mark the rune, use your preferred method, whether painting, engraving, or another technique. Treat this as an intentional process, focusing on the meaning of the Sickle rune as you work.

When finished, your Sickle stone can serve as an anchor for meditations, a point of focus in your practice, and a part of your divination work. As you progress through the exercises in this chapter, keep the rune nearby to strengthen your connection to the Sickle's themes of death, harvest, and transformation.

In Thought

It is important to get familiar with the Sickle rune symbol before undertaking the meditations in this section. Once you can clearly visualise the Sickle rune with your eyes closed, you can move on to the first meditation. The second meditation is longer, so you might like to record yourself reading the script and listen back so you can be fully present in the meditation.

Meditation 1: Exploring the Sickle Stone

The following meditation is unscripted and will help you build a connection with the image of the rune. The objective is to notice any existing concepts or associations that this rune might hold for you. By performing this exercise, you will be able to witness those ideas bubbling to the surface. Take note of anything that comes up and remember there is no right or wrong here. Spend some time recording anything that comes up in your journal when you are done.

Get into a comfortable position. Close your eyes and take several calming breaths. Take a moment here to check in with your body and to relax any spots where you feel tension. Let your breath dissolve and carry away any stress as your body grows soft and relaxed. Spend a minute or two here to settle into the exercise and set the intention to explore the symbol of this rune.

Now, with your eyes still closed, see the symbol of the Sickle. See it as clearly as you can, holding it in your imagination. You do not have to do anything else, simply regard the symbol and be open to insights. Take note of anything that comes up for you during this time, what thoughts, ideas, memories bubble up? Are there particular ideas that come to you? Body sensations? Take note of these things while letting your attention remain gently resting on the symbol of the Sickle.

If you happen to notice that your focus has wandered away to something else, tenderly bring your attention back to the symbol. Try to remain in this meditation for at least ten minutes.

You might like to perform this meditation several times as you work with this rune. You can also revisit it periodically to integrate new insights as your relationship grows.

Meditation 2: Meeting the Spirit of the Sickle Rune

This is the more in-depth meditation. The objective here is to go on a journey to meet the spirit of the Sickle rune so that you can build a relationship with it. This has two secondary benefits: The first is the ability to learn directly from the rune spirit, and the second is to anchor that spirit in your rune stone. You might like to record this script and play it back, perhaps with some calming music, or otherwise memorise the steps and walk yourself through the meditation. Be sure to leave adequate time at the marked pauses for interactions and input from beings within the meditation.

Begin by finding a comfortable position and closing your eyes. Take several deep, calming breaths, and let your body relax.

Take a deep breath in... and as you exhale, let go of any tension in your body. Allow yourself to settle into this moment, leaving behind any distractions or concerns. With each breath, feel yourself becoming more relaxed, more at ease.

Now, imagine yourself standing in a beautiful forest. The air is cool and fresh, and the sound of leaves rustling in the gentle breeze surrounds you. Sunlight filters through the canopy above, casting a soft dappled light onto the forest floor.

Take a moment to feel the soil beneath your feet. The earth is solid, grounding you. Each breath you take connects you more deeply with this peaceful place.

As you walk through the forest, you notice a large, ancient tree ahead of you. Its trunk is wide and strong, its bark thick and textured. There's something magical about this tree—it's as though it has been standing here for centuries, watching over the forest.

You feel drawn to the tree. As you get closer, you notice something remarkable: There is a doorway in the trunk of the tree. It's small and rounded, just

large enough for you to step through. The door itself is made of smooth wood, with intricate carvings that seem to shimmer slightly in the sunlight.

Take a moment to observe this doorway. What does it look like? Notice the details, the carvings, the way it feels as you gently reach out and touch it.

Now, when you're ready, place your hand on the door's handle. It opens easily, inviting you to step inside. Take a deep breath, and with your next exhale, step through the doorway.

As you pass through, you enter a new space. This place is calm and safe, a sanctuary just for you. Perhaps it's a beautiful garden, a peaceful meadow, or a cosy room—whatever feels right to you. Take a moment to explore this space. Feel the peace that surrounds you. You are safe here, and everything you need is already within you.

Breathe in deeply and let yourself relax even further. In this place, you are free from any worries or stress. Feel the calm washing over you, nurturing and restoring your mind and body.

Take some time here, in this space of peace and tranquillity. You can return to this place anytime you wish, simply by stepping through the doorway in the tree.

As you stand in your peaceful space, you feel a shift in the air around you. The energy becomes still and calm, as if something profound is about to unfold. In the distance, you see the outline of a large sickle—its curved blade gleaming in the soft light, reflecting a quiet but powerful presence.

The sickle stands as a symbol of endings, of cutting down what no longer serves, of making way for something new. It invites you to explore the meaning of completion, release, and transformation.

You feel drawn toward the sickle, knowing that it holds a message for you. As you approach, the landscape around you begins to shift and change, mirroring the cycles of life, death, and rebirth. The ground is soft beneath your feet, and the air carries a feeling of inevitability, reminding you that all things come to an end in their time.

This is the Sickle rune. It represents death, not just as a literal ending but as a moment of profound change—where something must be cut away or let go of in order to make space for growth and renewal. Take a moment to stand before this rune, feeling its solemn energy, the quiet power it holds, and the deep wisdom that lies in accepting endings.

The Sickle rune teaches you that in life, there are times to release, to cut away what no longer serves you, and to honour the natural cycles of completion. It reminds you that all endings are also beginnings and that letting go is an essential part of moving forward.

Breathe deeply, allowing the energy of the Sickle rune to move through you. Feel its quiet strength, its invitation to reflect on the parts of your life that may be ready to end, and its reminder that releasing is a part of renewal.

As you stand in this sacred space, you become aware of another presence nearby. This is the spirit of the Sickle rune, a guide who embodies the energy of endings, release, and transformation. The spirit approaches you with a quiet, grounded energy, carrying the wisdom of cycles and the inevitability of change.

The spirit of the Sickle rune may appear as a hooded figure, cloaked in the colours of the earth, or as an energy that feels grounded and final, like the close of a chapter. Allow the spirit to take whatever form feels natural to you.

As the spirit draws near, you feel a sense of calm acceptance, knowing that this spirit is here to guide you through the process of release. It is not a force of destruction, but of clearing—helping you to see what must be cut away so that you can grow. The Sickle rune teaches that endings are not to be feared but embraced as part of the natural flow of life.

Take a moment to connect with the spirit of the Sickle rune. Feel its energy of closure, acceptance, and peace. This spirit embodies the understanding that some things in life must end and that releasing them is an act of strength and wisdom. It is here to help you identify what may need to be let go of in your life and how to do so with grace.

The spirit now invites you to reflect on an area of your life where an ending may be needed. Perhaps there is a situation, relationship, or belief that no longer serves you—something that you've been holding on to even though it may be time to release it. Take a moment to reflect on this, and when you are ready, silently or aloud, ask the spirit of the Sickle rune to guide you in this process of letting go.

(Pause for reflection.)

The spirit may respond with a feeling of clarity, showing you what needs to be cut away, or with a sense of peace, helping you to release any fear or resistance around this ending. It might give you a deeper understanding of why this release is necessary or help you see the new space it will create for growth and renewal. Trust whatever comes to you, even if it feels subtle or gentle. The Sickle rune teaches us that endings, though sometimes difficult, are always followed by transformation.

Take a moment to sit with the guidance you've received. Feel how the energy of the Sickle rune supports you in the process of letting go, helping you to honour what has ended and to make space for what will come next.

Now, the spirit offers you a final message—a gift of wisdom or peace as you continue on your journey of release and renewal. Open your heart and mind to receive this final message.

(Pause briefly.)

As your time with the spirit of the Sickle rune comes to an end, you feel a deep sense of acceptance and peace. The spirit begins to withdraw, like the quiet fading of day into night, but the feeling of release and transformation remains, filling the space with calm and clarity.

Take a deep breath, knowing that you can return to this space and this spirit whenever you need to release something in your life. The energy of the Sickle rune is always within you, guiding you through the natural cycles of endings and beginnings and reminding you that letting go is a part of growth.

Now, turn away from the rune and begin to walk back toward the doorway in the tree. As you move through your peaceful space, you carry the quiet strength of the Sickle rune with you, knowing that its energy will continue to guide you through moments of release and transformation.

Step through the doorway once again, returning to the forest. Feel the solid ground beneath your feet, hear the gentle rustling of the leaves in the breeze, and sense the stillness of the forest as you return to the present.

With each breath, bring yourself back to the present moment. Begin to notice your body again, feeling the surface beneath you, the air on your skin.

When you are ready, gently open your eyes, feeling calm, clear, and connected to the energy of release and transformation.

When you have finished, take a moment to record your insights: What did you see? What have you learnt? Did anything surprise you?

As part of your records, you can sketch out any particularly vivid imagery that came through your meditation as a way of grounding it into the physical world.

You might also like to try a grounding exercise to help bring you back to the present moment. This can be achieved by standing barefoot on the earth, imagining energetic roots reaching from your feet into the ground and balancing your energy, or resting your forehead on the floor for a moment.

In Words

Reflect on your ideas about death. Do you think it has a moral aspect? Does it generate strong emotions? Do you want to avoid thinking about it? Explore these reactions and try to understand them.

Contemplate the role of death in the continuity of life. Your body is sustained by the death of plants and animals, soil is formed of the decayed matter of previously living things, and all living things will eventually die. Consider the inseparable nature of these two forces and observe any impressions or emotions that come up.

In what ways have endings or losses been transformative for you? How can you embrace this symbolism of cutting away to create positive change in your life?

How did the process of reaping and sowing feel? What did you learn about the balance between endings and beginnings, and how might that shift your current understanding of cycles in your life?

Don't forget to record your experiences and insights from the exercises in this chapter. Taking the time to journal your responses to the activities and prompts will help to clarify your own understanding and relationship to the symbol of the Sickle rune. You can also write out your own interpretation of the rune, incorporating everything you have learnt from the process of exploring the symbolism and making your own Sickle rune.

Chapter Thirteen
MAKING YOUR STONES

While it is of course possible to purchase a set of Witches' Runes, crafting your own is a process steeped in both practicality and intention, a practice as much about method as it is about meaning. Engraving symbols onto stones, whether with a simple line or a carefully etched design, invites you to explore the medium's physical and spiritual possibilities.

Making Your Mark

We already discussed methods and considerations for selecting your stones in chapter 2, but do they have to be a specific type of stone? Could other materials be used? In our time working with and teaching this system, we have come across sets made of stone, burned or painted onto wooden discs, made out of natural or polymer clay, and more. There are no hard-and-fast rules governing what your set should be made of, but common sense should dictate that your stones aren't so brittle or fragile that they crumble when they knock together. Your whole set should fit comfortably in your cupped hands, and each stone should have at least two clear planes so that they can land face down or face up without rolling.

Selecting your method for marking these stones—be it through engraving, painting, or inlay— shapes the connection between you and each rune, imbuing the stones with your own energy and skill.

Before you begin, consider both the qualities of the materials you are drawn to and the level of permanence you wish to achieve. Some techniques yield rugged, timeless marks, while others add colour or shimmer, capturing the essence of each rune in a way that speaks uniquely to you. As you decide on a method, approach each step with care, knowing that in crafting these runes, you are creating a tool for divination, meditation, and connection with the deeper currents of meaning within and around you.

Here we will share several methods you could use to mark your stones, depending on the look you want and the tools you have available. You might want to use different methods for different runes or create a cohesive set using one process. It is also possible to have more than one set, and you might like to begin with a simpler method before crafting a more elaborate set as your relationship with the runes deepens.

Painting and Image Transfer

Again, there are several approaches to this that are available to you depending on your skill level and tools. Always follow a manufacturer's recommendations around the wearing of gloves or other safety gear.

Acrylic Paints

For detailed designs, use waterproof acrylic paints with fine-tipped brushes.

Process

1. Clean the stone to remove dust and grease.
2. Sketch your symbol lightly with a pencil.
3. Use small brushes to apply acrylic paint to your design.
4. Let the pain dry fully, then seal with a clear waterproof varnish for durability.

Paint Pens or Markers

These allow for precision and are available in various colours. Make sure they're oil-based for longevity.

Process

1. Prepare the stone as previously instructed.
2. Use permanent markers or oil-based paint pens for a steady application.
3. Seal with a varnish to protect the paint.

Decoupage or Image Transfer

Decoupage is an easy method to use and great for more intricate designs, but it will also impact the tactile experience of the stone. As they will require several coats of glue to finish, the stones can end up feeling overly slippery, shiny, or artificial. You will need a clear-drying glue, such as Mod Podge, and a brush to apply it, scissors, and thin paper.

Process

1. Prepare the stone as previously instructed.
2. Print or draw your design on thin paper.
3. Cut around the design and apply a layer of clear-drying glue to the stone.
4. Place the paper design onto the glue and smooth it out to remove air bubbles.
5. Apply another layer of glue over the top.
6. Let it dry completely and seal for longevity.

Metal Leaf or Foil Transfer

This method involves etching a shallow design, then using metal leaf or foil to create a metallic, embossed look. You'll need a carving tool, such as an engraving pen, an adhesive, such as craft glue or Mod Podge, a soft brush, and your desired metal leaf or foil. A pair of tweezers is recommended for placement.

Process

1. Prepare the stone as previously instructed.
2. Carve your symbol shallowly into the stone.
3. Apply adhesive designed for metal leaf along the carved area.
4. Press the metal leaf onto the adhesive. Use gold, silver, or copper leaf for a metallic look.
5. Use a soft brush to remove excess leaf around the symbol.
6. Seal the leaf with a clear varnish to protect it from tarnishing.

Airbrush

Using an airbrush is great for achieving smoother gradients or elaborate designs. With this method, it's crucial to apply a fixative or varnish afterward. You'll need to make a stencil of your design to place on the stone, an airbrush kit with suitable paint designed for airbrushes, and a sealant.

Process

1. Prepare the stone as previously instructed.
2. Create a stencil of your design to place on the stone.
3. Set up the airbrush and carefully spray over the stencil.
4. Let dry and seal to keep the colours vibrant.

Engraving

There are multiple ways you can approach engraving a stone. When engraving stone, always be safe around dust: Work in a well-ventilated spot, wear a mask, and follow the manufacturer's advice—sometimes this might include having water handy to rinse your stones or even "working wet" for dust prevention.

Hand Engraving

You will need a handheld rotary tool, such as a Dremel, with an engraving tip to carve the symbol into the stone, a soft brush, and, if desired, a stone-friendly varnish. This method provides a more permanent marking than painting or drawing.

Process

1. Prepare the stone as previously instructed.
2. Clean and dry the stone surface.
3. Sketch your symbol with a pencil or use a stencil.
4. Attach an engraving bit to the rotary tool.
5. Begin carving, applying light pressure and guiding the tool over your design.
6. Clean off dust with a soft brush, then optionally seal with a stone-friendly varnish.

Engraving Pen

Follow the steps for the hand engraving method, using a stone engraving pen instead for more precise control. A stone engraving pen is an engraving pen specialised for use with stone that can give you control for intricate designs.

Hammer and Chisel

This traditional method works well on harder and larger stones, allowing you to create deep carvings for long-lasting effects. The nature of this method makes it less suitable for smaller stones.

Process

1. Prepare the stone as previously instructed.
2. Use a pencil to draw the symbol or tape a stencil onto the stone.
3. Place the chisel at the edge of your design and tap gently with a hammer to begin carving.
4. Move along the design in small sections to control chipping.
5. Dust off debris and seal, if desired.

Again, this is not necessarily recommended for smaller stones but could be a useful method for crafting larger versions of the runes for use in magic.

Inlaying

The inlaying effect is created by pouring resin, sometimes with crushed stones or powdered metal, into an image carved into the stone. You'll need a carving tool of some kind as well as some resin, optional coloured or crushed stone powder, sandpaper, and a sealant.

Process

1. Prepare the stone as previously instructed.
2. Carve a shallow outline of your design using a rotary tool or engraving pen.
3. Mix the resin with a colour or crushed stone powder if using.
4. Fill the carved area with resin and smooth it out.
5. Let the resin cure fully, then sand down to reveal the image and smooth away any uneven areas.
6. Seal for a polished finish.

Pyrography (Stone Burning)

Some stones, particularly softer ones such as soapstone, can be marked with a woodburning tool, which is a bit like a soldering iron and can be picked up from craft shops or bought online. It's a good idea to do a few tests on different types of stone to ensure your selected stones will be soft enough for this method. This is more challenging but can create unique effects. You'll need a woodburning tool and safety gloves. If you're working with wood and prefer a raw, natural look, don't worry about varnish. Varnish will, however, give your runes a longer life if they are to be handled a lot and will protect them from getting grimy from use.

Process

1. Prepare the stone as previously instructed.
2. Clean the stone surface.
3. Draw the design lightly with a pencil.
4. Use a woodburning tool (only on soft stones!) to slowly "burn" the design.
5. Move in gentle strokes, allowing the tool to leave dark marks as desired.
6. Clean the surface of any residue and optionally seal with varnish.

Laser Engraving

If you have access to a laser engraver, it can mark most stones very precisely, depending on the type of stone and the laser's power. Again, it is a good idea to do a few test pieces before embarking on engraving your runes.

Process

1. Prepare the stone as previously instructed.
2. Set up the laser engraver and prepare the design in the machine's software.
3. Position the stone correctly under the laser.
4. Adjust the laser settings (such as power and speed) depending on the stone's hardness.
5. Start the engraving process and allow the machine to complete the design.
6. Clean off residue and, if desired, apply a sealant.

Sandblasting

If you have access to a sandblasting kit, you can use a stencil to blast the symbol onto the stone. This method is commonly used for headstones or signs and is long lasting. You will need stencil material or painter's tape, a cutting tool, a sandblasting kit, a soft brush, and a sealant.

Process

1. Prepare the stone as previously instructed.
2. Cover the stone with stencil material or painter's tape.
3. Cut out your symbol shape, exposing only where you want the symbol to be etched.
4. Sandblast the exposed area using a gentle, controlled spray.
5. Clean off the sand residue with the soft brush and remove the stencil.
6. Apply a sealant to enhance durability.

Etching with Chemicals

Acid etching is a highly effective method for engraving symbols onto certain stones, such as limestone and marble, or metals. However, results may vary depending on the stone's composition and porosity. This method involves using a diluted acid—such as muriatic acid or ferric chloride—along with a stencil to create a permanent etched design. Since acids can be hazardous to human health, it is crucial to take all necessary precautions when working with them. Wear goggles, gloves, and clothes that cover your arms and body. Work in a well-ventilated space, ensure your surfaces are nonreactive (usually plastic works, but this will also depend on the acid in use, so talk to your vendor), and have an abundant supply of water on hand as well as a neutralising substance, such as bicarbonate of soda.

Required Materials

- *Protective gear:* Acid-resistant gloves, safety goggles, and a face mask.
- *Stone surface:* Limestone, marble, or other acid-sensitive stone.
- *Cleaning supplies:* Mild soap, water, and a clean cloth.
- *Stencil material:* Vinyl stencil, adhesive stencil, or masking tape to cover areas not to be etched.
- *Application brush:* Acid-resistant brush or swab.

- *Properly diluted acid:* An acid, such as muriatic acid or ferric chloride, prepared following manufacturer's instructions.
- *Water supply:* A hose, bucket of clean water, or spray bottle for rinsing.
- *Neutralising compound:* Bicarbonate of soda (baking soda) or similar base to neutralise the acid.
- *Tool for final cleaning and finishing:* Soft brush or cloth.

Process

1. Before starting, put on all necessary protective gear: gloves, goggles, and mask. Ensure you are working in a well-ventilated area or outdoors. Safety first! Keep your neutralising compound and plenty of water nearby in case of spills and for step 5.
2. Prepare the stone by thoroughly cleaning it with mild soap and water to remove any dirt or residue that might interfere with the acid etching process. Allow the stone to dry completely before proceeding.
3. Place your stencil securely onto the stone, ensuring it adheres well and exposes only the design area you want to etch. If using masking tape, press down firmly to create clean edges.
4. Using an acid-resistant brush or swab, carefully apply the diluted acid to the exposed areas of the stencil. Allow the acid to react with the stone for the recommended time—typically a few minutes—but always follow the manufacturer's specific instructions. Some people will have a small basin of the acid solution and tape the stone so that it rests face down on the surface to react. If using this approach, be sure to check the depth of the etch periodically.
5. Neutralise the surface to stop any remaining acid reaction by applying a baking soda solution (mix a few tablespoons of baking soda with water) over the etched area. This will neutralise any lingering acid. Be aware that there will often be a reaction and foaming as the chemical reaction takes place. Be very careful not to mix large amounts of acid and neutralising compounds rapidly as this can cause overflow and rapid gas release. If using a neutralising bath for the stone, ensure there is no undissolved bicarb on the bottom of the container as this will react aggressively should any acid be dropped into the container.

6. Be sure to rinse the stone thoroughly with plenty of clean water to clear away any residues. Avoid splashing and ensure the surface is clean.
7. Carefully peel off the stencil and inspect the etching. Use a soft brush or cloth to gently clean the surface and remove any debris.
8. Allow the stone to dry completely. If desired, apply a sealant to enhance contrast and protect the etched design.
9. Dispose of any remaining solution. If you use the acid bath method, gradually dilute and neutralise the used acid before disposing. You do not want to pour active acids down your pipes or allow it to contact any metal surfaces, as this could cause corrosion.

Choosing Your Method

Each of these methods will create a different aesthetic. Choosing one depends on the materials you have and the effect you want. Don't be afraid to experiment and explore each method prior to fashioning your rune set in order to get familiar with the technique. Diving into the process of working with stones in this way opens up a range of other experiences related to ancestral ties and building relationships with stones in a more tangible (dare we say, animist?) fashion.

Chapter Fourteen
Reading the Runes

Once you have your consecrated set of stones, made or purchased, and you've connected to each symbol through meditation or ritual, you are ready to start reading. Readings for the Witches' Runes are performed in two ways, either by placing the Eye stone face up and holding the other nine stones in both hands or by keeping the Eye stone with the others and holding all ten. The reader then chants, blows on the stones, and casts or drops them onto and around the Eye stone if they are reading with that stone signifying the querent. Any stones that lie face down are set aside, and the remaining stones are interpreted in a spiral pattern, reading outwards from the Eye stone if it's being used to represent the querent.

We will now go over both reading methods.

Reading with the Eye as Querent

This first method uses the Eye stone to represent the subject of the reading. You will read with only nine stones. This is the way we were originally taught to read the runes. This method is commonly found in books about the Witches' Runes, and it is also the way of reading favoured by Ashcroft-Nowicki.[112]

The Method

You'll need a flat space, such as a tabletop, to read your runes, just as you would other stones or cards. It is considered good magical hygiene—as well as good everyday hygiene—to ensure the surface is free of dust, crumbs, and other materials.

112. Ashcroft-Nowicki, "The Gypsy Runes."

1. Place the Eye face up in front of you. Allow space for the stones to fall as they may all around the Eye: Leave room above, below, to the left, and to the right of it.
2. Still your mind and visualise the question you have. If you're reading for somebody else, look at the person and try to really perceive them and how they occupy the space in front of you.
3. Recite the chant over the stones in your hands. The following chant is from Ashcroft-Nowicki's article and is more or less the same as the chant we were taught when we learned about these stones; ours has variations in the last few lines.

Stones O'Leary,
Stones O'Leary,
tell me truly,
tell me clearly,
give to me an answer true,
show me what I am to do.
Let my Eye see clear and bright
that I may keep my future right.[113]

4. Blow air onto the stones in your cupped hands. This is thought to wake them up and strengthen their connection with you, the reader.
5. Cast the stones. Open your hands to drop all the stones onto and around the Eye stone in one movement.
6. Discard any stones lying face down. Stones without symbols showing are not part of this reading. Put them aside and focus only on the stones lying face up.
7. Read the remaining stones in a spiral, starting at the stone closest to the Eye stone. Use the correspondences you have learned from working through the activities in previous chapters to help you interpret the stones. Later in this chapter, there is a handy list to help you understand combinations of certain stones that may appear, and a quick refence guide can be found in the appendix.

---

113. Ashcroft-Nowicki, "The Gypsy Runes," 234.

In time, and as you work with your own set of stones, you will come to have your own associations with certain stones and patterns of stones too.

Leading Stone

When you read with the nine-stone method, you will usually have a *leading* stone, a stone that falls closest to the Eye stone. There is usually only one of these. This is generally the most prominent factor, influence, or energy in the reading. Stones in the leading position take more prominence in meaning than if they were further back.

Being the leading stone sometimes alters that stones' divinatory meaning slightly. Some ways to interpret leading stones are as follows.

- If your leading stone is the *Sun*, it usually points to a favourable outcome or positive times ahead. If there is only one other stone in the reading, that thing should be viewed in a favourable, fortunate way.
- The *Moon* in the leading position can sometimes point to a change of position or outlook over the next twenty-eight days. Tread carefully.
- If the *Rings* rune appears as the leading stone, it's usually an affirmative answer to questions about someone's affections, or a speedy affair, marriage, or engagement.
- The *Birds* in flight as the leading stone points to some life-changing news for the querent, usually positive.
- If the leading stone is the *Waves*, the querent's family has some influence over the matter at hand.
- The *Wheat* stone is considered incredibly lucky if it is the stone closest to the Eye stone.
- When the leading stone is the *Crossed Spears*, there is strife not far away.

Reading with Ten Stones

Some people prefer not to use the Eye stone to represent the querent, instead including it with the other nine as they are tossed. This method is favoured by Crowther in her book *Lid Off the Cauldron*.

The Method

When reading in this way, you follow the same process outlined previously without separating out any stone from the set. In this case, however, the Eye rune is not a centre point for contextualising the reading; it is simply a rune within the set just like any other. It represents the focus of the querent and the runes nearest it (or directly in its line of sight) represent obstructions, distractions, or the object of focus for the querent.

As with the nine-stone reading, you'll need a flat space, such as a tabletop, to read your runes. Ensure that it is clean and free of clutter. Then follow these steps.

1. Still your mind and visualise the question you have. If you're reading for somebody else, look at the person and try to really perceive them and how they occupy the space in front of you.
2. Recite the chant over the stones in your hands. The following chant is from the Ashcroft-Nowicki article and is similar to the chant we were taught when we learned about these stones; ours has variations in the last few lines.

   Stones O'Leary,
   Stones O'Leary,
   tell me truly,
   tell me clearly,
   give to me an answer true,
   show me what I am to do.
   Let my Eye see clear and bright
   that I may keep my future right.[114]

3. Blow air onto the stones in your cupped hands. This is thought to wake them up and strengthen their connection with you, the reader.
4. Cast the stones. Open your hands to drop all the stones in one movement.

114. Ashcroft-Nowicki, "The Gypsy Runes," 234.

5. Discard any stones lying face down. Stones without symbols showing are not part of this reading. Put them aside and focus only on the stones lying face up.
6. Read the remaining stones. There are several schools of thought on the order of significance. In one way of thinking, the closest stone to you is the most significant or nearest in the timeline. The stones that fall further away grow further away in time and significance. Conversely, some people interpret the toss with the stone furthest from you being the most significant and nearest in time or of highest importance. Go with what makes sense to you.

In time, and as you work with your own set of stones, you will come to have your own associations with certain stones and patterns of stones too. You might also consider the Eye stone to be "you" and count the order of significance from that. Use the correspondences you have learned from working through the activities in previous chapters to help you interpret the stones. Later in this chapter, there is a handy list to help you understand combinations of certain stones that may appear, and a quick refence guide can be found in the appendix.

Points to Remember

Following are some handy tips to help you get started and feeling confident reading with this system.

Keep Questions Simple

Keeping your queries simple is essential, especially when you're starting out. Word the questions carefully. You might have more luck as a beginner if you ask closed questions, such as those where you are looking for a clear yes-or-no answer. If you're not sure what the answer to a yes-or-not question is in a reading, look for what you have more of. Traditionally positive and favourable stones, such as the Sun, Harvest, and Star, can be taken as a yes, and stones more often associated with caution and things as yet unseen, such as the Sickle, Crossed Spears, and Moon, can indicate a no in the right circumstances.

Stones That Fall Face Down Are Not Included

As we mentioned earlier, stones that fall face down are mute and not speaking in that reading. Set them aside for the reading and pay attention to the face-up stones only.

When All Stones Appear Face Down

If all stones appear face down, discontinue the reading. Try again once some time has passed. This is usually a sign to take a break and to give the stones a break too. Put them back into their bag and let them rest for a few days at least.

Stacked Stones

If two stones land on top of each other and are both face up, they both should be read. This, in fact, is where the answer to your question lies. Read it as such.

Watch for Certain Combinations

There are some combinations of stones that, when appearing together and especially next to each other, have certain meanings. You will come to recognise these with time and practice, and as you go, you'll notice that some stones seem to gravitate to one another and appear together frequently. The following list shows you the meaning of significant combinations.

- *Sun/Moon:* A sudden change towards the positive in events.
- *Sun/Birds:* Important messages or gossip coming to you from a distance.
- *Sun/Waves:* A long journey.
- *Sun/Wheat:* The birth of something new.
- *Sun/Crossed Spears:* Watch out for treachery, obstacles, or opposition.
- *Sun/Star:* Represents the querent's hopes and dreams.
- *Moon/Rings:* Your question may no longer be relevant.
- *Moon/Birds:* A sudden and serious illness.
- *Moon/Waves:* An accident or illness.
- *Moon/Sickle:* A prompt to resolve an issue from your childhood.
- *Rings/Waves:* A romance will take the querent abroad.
- *Rings/Wheat:* A business partnership or a wealthy marriage.
- *Rings/Crossed Spears:* The healing or revival of a troubled partnership.
- *Birds/Wheat:* Messages that bring joy or good news from friends far away.

- *Waves/Star:* Birth of a child in the querent's family.
- *Waves/Sickle:* Someone close to the querent will move away.
- *Wheat/Crossed Spears:* The healing of a quarrel.
- *Crossed Spears/Sickle:* A serious argument or falling out.

Don't Cast Frivolously

Multiple sources, including Ashcroft-Nowicki and Crowther, stress not to cast stones frivolously. It's best to save this system as something you bring out when you have a pressing, serious question or need clarification on a question or answer of this nature. Casting the stones carelessly or without a real reason can affect the relationship you have with your unique and personalised set.

Be Careful Whom You Let Handle Your Runes

This is good advice, applicable to any number of divinatory tools, but lore around these stones in particular suggests they're not to be handled by too many people—and especially not strangers. Crowther takes this further, suggesting that in giving your stones to someone else you will cause them to "never again tell a true story."[115]

Sample Readings with Nine Stones

The following readings were performed by us to answer actual questions and for specific purposes. In these cases, we used nine stones, and the Eye stone represented the querent. In this method, it is always at the centre of the reading and read as representing the subject of the reading rather than a divinatory sign.

For each reading, we have provided a description of the stones' positions before providing a commentary. As someone getting to know this system, it would be a useful exercise to try your hand at interpreting these readings yourself, then comparing your notes to our interpretation.

We've only listed the stones that fell face up in each reading. After the commentary, we'll bring together the interpretations and come to a conclusion, including any possible actions we think the querent should take.

115. Crowther, *Lid Off the Cauldron*, 114.

Question: Should I Start Looking for a New Job?

Fed up with some of the aspects of their current job, a client asked whether they should look for a new job or stick it out where they are working at the moment.

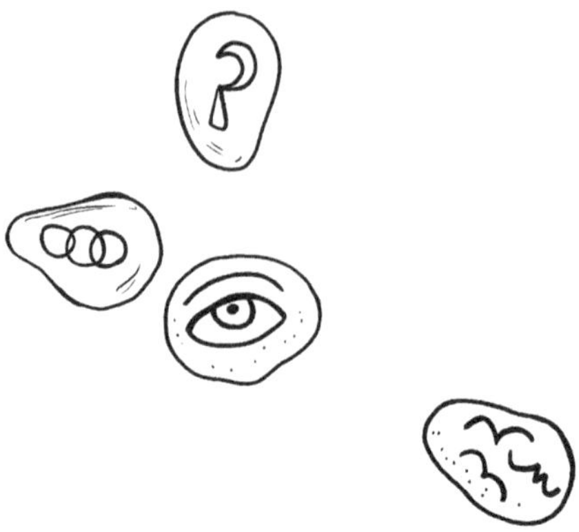

Stone Layout

In order from closest to the Eye to furthest away: Rings, Sickle, Birds. The spiral moves to the left.

Commentary

In this reading, the Rings stone is almost touching the Eye. It speaks of bonds already forged with coworkers and others at their current workplace. The Sickle warns that this person seems quite hasty to leave their current employer and suggests that this will be an abrupt ending that may not be undone; quitting now would certainly burn some bridges at the person's current workplace. The Birds speak of accessing a lot of information and communication. Their distance from the Eye tells us that this is information overload... so much so that it can be overwhelming for this person to make a decision, and when they do, discernment can be tricky.

Conclusion and Actions

The Rings stone speaks of the significance of the established bonds between the subject of this reading and the people they currently work with. The Birds stone warns that to move hastily on applying for other positions could be interpreted or communicated the wrong way, and the Sickle hints at the possibility this could cause damage to—or even end—these relationships.

With no specific plan for what they would do if they left their current position, this person has given themselves an "information overload" with all of the options available to them. The immediate way forward is not immediately clear, but there is a caution here to look before one leaps.

Question: Will This Family Member Recover Quickly? Will Their Health Be Okay?

The querent here has a close family member recovering from major surgery. This family member, who is usually quite active and leads a busy life, has been recommended lots of rest and no driving or strenuous activity for a couple of months as they recover.

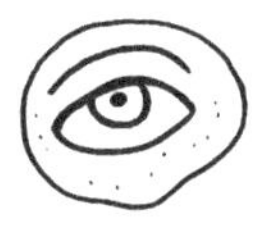

Stone Layout

In order from closest to the Eye to furthest away: Sickle, Wheat, Rings, Waves. The spiral moves to the left.

Commentary

The Sickle so close to the Eye here might initially look like cause for alarm, but when we consider this surgery had to do with someone's reproductive health and the Sickle immediately precedes the Wheat, a picture begins to form. In this case, there has been a *literal* cutting away related to fertility and childbirth. The Sickle and the Wheat sit on either side of the Eye, almost like the two sides of a set of scales. There is a balance to be struck here with regards to this person's healing journey, an implication that there are two ways this could go.

The Rings stone speaks of close relationships and the Waves of movement and travel. We know that this person has had offers of help from family members, and these family members do not live in the same place as them.

Conclusion and Actions

The balanced positions of the Sickle and the Wheat stones hint at two possible directions this healing could take: one of difficulties and endings/changes to the current status quo and one of health and abundance. The Rings stone speaks of close bonds to one or more people, and when combined with the Waves, it means these people are not necessarily as close in physical proximity as they are in their care for one another. This person will have a fairly smooth healing journey IF they can find the time and humility to take up close family and friends on their offers of care.

Question: How Will We Fare Between Now and the Summer Solstice?

In late October here in the Southern Hemisphere, we celebrate Beltane, one of eight sabbats on the Wiccan Wheel of the Year. This reading was performed to gauge the vibe of the next six weeks overall for us and those closest to us. The period between Beltane and the Summer Solstice in this part of the world tends to get quite busy: The weather has warmed up, and there are often more Pagan and witchy events that we and many of our friends attend or organise. There's also the end of the school and university year for those of us studying, and the festive season in December and January means lots of family events both magical and mundane—and the travel associated with these.

Stone Layout

In order from closest to the Eye to furthest away: Star. The spiral moves to the left.

Commentary

The ambitious, hopeful Star stone appearing as the only stone in the reading is a very positive sign indeed. It encourages us to keep our dreams and ambitions at the fore, even in the upcoming busier mundane times. It is a nudge to keep up with creative and passion projects and to continue to follow what brings us joy and inspiration, to draw energy from these endeavours when we're feeling flat or frazzled from the more hectic end of the year, and also to feed these endeavours with the appropriate amounts of energy.

Conclusion and Actions

The star on its own speaks to our ambitions and the creative, fruitful energy of the Beltane season. Undisturbed by any other stones, it is a clear nudge to stay the course, to follow our passions, and to keep doing whatever it is that we're doing that is positive and inspiring and good. As Doreen Valiente says in her famous poem "The Charge of the Goddess," "Keep pure your highest ideal; strive ever toward it; let naught stop you or turn you aside."[116] The overall feeling for this reading is very positive—with the added implication that there may be work to do on our creative and passion projects.

116. Valiente, *Charge of the Goddess*, 12–13.

Question: Is Next Year a Good Time for Me to Travel Overseas for the First Time?

The querent of this reading is a nervous traveller wondering if next year is a good time to travel overseas for the first time.

Stone Layout

In order from closest to the Eye to furthest away: Waves, Star, Wheat, Moon, Birds, Crossed Spears. The spiral moves to the left.

Commentary

When in the position of the leading stone, the Waves stone is usually a reference to the querent's family and the influence they have over the life and decisions of the querent. As the Star is the very next stone along the Waves, we can interpret the two stones together as speaking about a birth—of a child, an idea, or something else—close to the querent. The abundant, fruitful Wheat stone appears next in the spiral, and even though the Crossed Spears stone is the last stone, it sits closest to the Wheat stone. In combination with the Wheat, it speaks of a rift or quarrel—often one that is long-standing—being healed. The Crossed Spears are the furthest from the Eye and not near any other stones other than the Wheat. This is a very favourable sign.

Next along from the Wheat is the Moon, with its otherworldly hints of things yet unseen and yet to come to pass. Beside the Birds, it references an illness. The same is the case with the Waves, earlier on in the reading. The Birds appear next, speaking of travel, communication, and movement. Their presence along with the Waves in a reading asking explicitly about travel gives us good footing for answering the querent's question—or beginning to answer it.

Conclusion and Actions

As is often the case with this system, the answer to this question is more of a "yes, but…" than a "yes, definitely." The presence of both the Birds and the Waves in different parts of the reading speaks of favourable travel, journeys, and good tidings from afar, but this isn't to say that things will be straightforward. With an unexpected illness somewhere close to the querent and a birth or beginning of something important and new—potentially stemming from a mended friendship or other relationship—they may have their hands full.

Our advice to this person was to go ahead with the travel if they desired to but to stay on top of their health and to be prepared for progress and travel plans to not always be linear.

Sample Readings with Ten Stones

In the following sample readings, the Eye stone is included and cast with the other nine stones. These readings are performed in a similar manner as they were in the last section, but instead of looking at the stones' proximity to the Eye stone to gauge levels of importance, the reader instead looks at the stones' proximity to the reader.

We have once again only listed the stones that fell face up in each reading. You will find a description of the stones' positions before our commentary. As we noted earlier, it is a useful exercise to try your hand at interpreting these readings yourself before seeing our own interpretations. Give it a try. After offering our commentary, we'll bring together the interpretations and come to a conclusion, including any possible actions we think the querent should take.

Question: Will I Find a Partner in the Next Twelve Months?

This reading was performed for a single person who asked about finding a romantic partner.

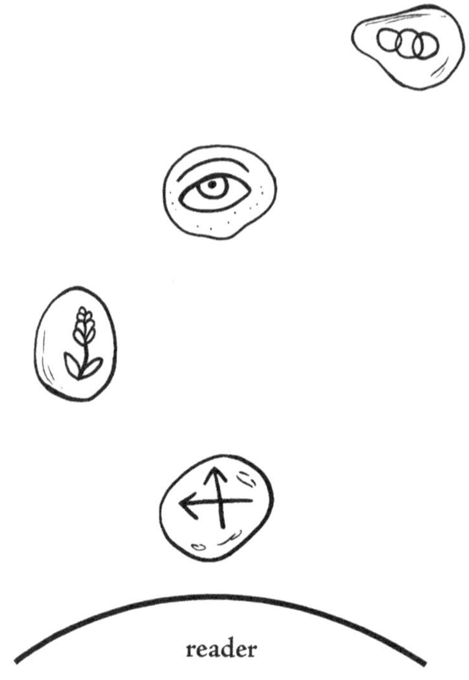

Stone Layout

In order from closest to the reader to furthest away: Crossed Spears (leading stone), Wheat, Eye, Rings.

Commentary

The Crossed Spears as the leading stone in this reading could be read as a warning of strife and trouble not far away, and also as a warning to wait before taking any drastic action. The Wheat stone immediately next in the reading speaks of the benefits or "fruits" of not rushing in. Indeed, the combination of the Crossed Spears and the Wheat stones often indicates the healing of a relationship: often a mending of fences after a long-standing quarrel. The Rings stone at the end of this reading is certainly a good omen and predicts a happy partnership—albeit a little far off just now—as does the combination of the Wheat and the Rings. The Eye positioned second to last in the reading places the querent somewhere between the quarrel/healing and the happy partnership.

Conclusion and Actions

The querent has probably already experienced the falling out hinted at by the Crossed Spears and the Wheat, but the Rings stone's prediction of a happy partnership is yet to come—and won't for a while. This points to someone the querent already knows: It might be a former lover, or perhaps the querent and a friend will make the decision to transform their friendship into something more. Either way, the querent is being prompted to look to those people already in their life before casting the net further.

Question: Is Now the Time to Launch into a New Creative Endeavour?

The subject of this reading is a creative person looking to launch into a new project. They asked the stones about the timing of this.

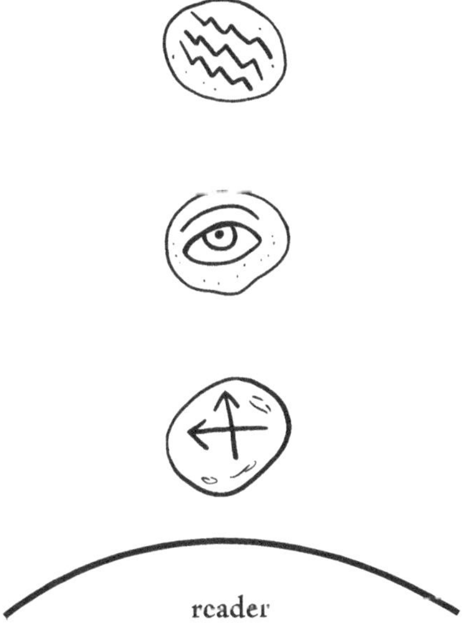

Stone Layout

In order from closest to the reader to furthest away: Crossed Spears (leading stone), Eye, Waves.

Commentary

This reading has the Crossed Spears as the leading stone, which feels like a very clear sign for the querent to stay their hand for now. The Waves stone sits in front of the Eye, indicating a fluid and changing situation for some time, and a situation that needs attention. The Crossed Spears stone sits just below the Eye, within its full sight.

Conclusion and Actions

Simply put, the answer is no, now is not the time to begin a new creative project. This simple combination with no other contributing stones tells us clearly that there are too many fluid, changing situations going on for the querent for them to have the available energy or time to put into a project and do it justice. We'll check back with this in a few months and see if anything has shifted.

Question: Should I Keep Trying to Get in Touch with this Friend? Will My Life Be Worse Off for No Longer Knowing Them?

This querent has lost touch with a longtime friend and former lover. Their relationship had not soured but dwindled as they both grew and changed as people. Now this friend does not answer this subject's attempts to make contact. Is it worth pursuing or time to let go?

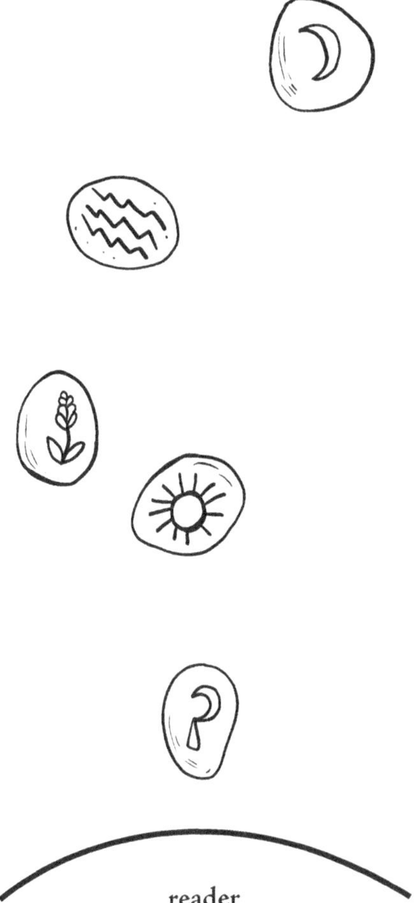

Stone Layout

In order from closest to the reader to furthest away: Sickle (leading stone), Sun, Wheat, Waves, Moon.

Commentary

The Sickle as leading stone sends a fairly clear message about endings, no matter how painful. The Sun and Wheat stones sit almost on top of each other behind the Sickle, together speaking of a new beginning or the birth of something new. The Waves and Moon sit further back again and speak of the underlying, unresolved emotions and intuitions that are at play in the background, which have been for a long time.

Conclusion and Actions

We could almost halt the reading at the first stone that appears: The Sickle speaks plainly here that letting go of this now one-sided interaction is best for the subject of this reading. The overwhelmingly positive pair of the Wheat and Sun stones sits behind this painful truth, promising of better things to come once they have moved on from what no longer serves them or brings them joy. The Moon and Waves let us know just how much emotion and energy the subject has put into turning this fizzled out friendship over and over in their head, but the intuitive Moon suggests—gently—that maybe the subject knew things had finished but they haven't been ready to accept it for some time.

Question: What Can I Do to Help Me Gain Employment That I'll Be Satisfied With, That Will Meet My Needs?

The subject of this reading is about to be made redundant and has had trouble in the past finding stable employment that suits their lifestyle and meets their needs. Instead of the more ambiguous "*will I find work?*" we shifted the focus to actions that would create the best possible conditions in which this person could find and succeed in a job or career.

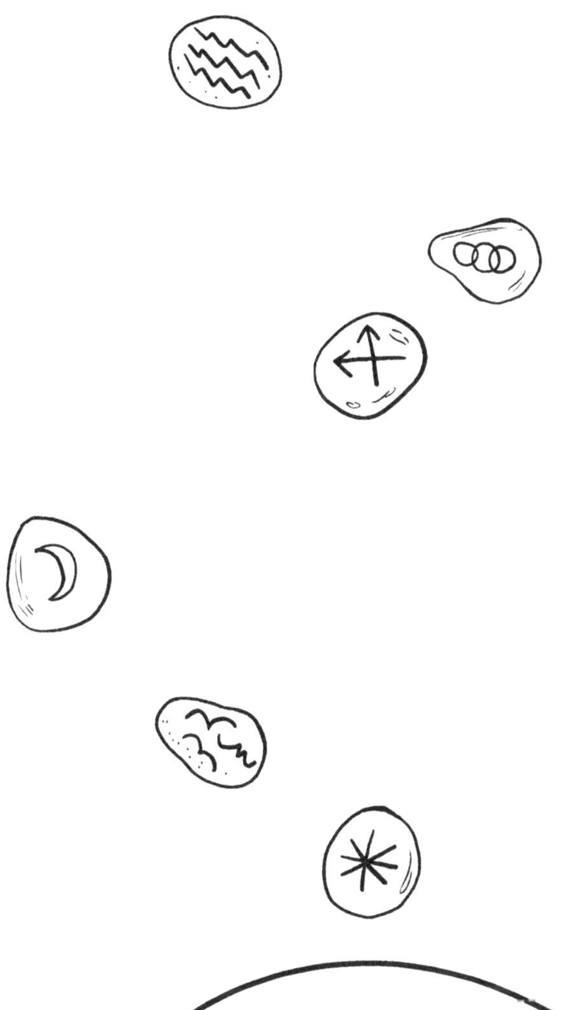

Stones Layout

In order from closest to the reader to furthest away: Star (leading stone), Birds, Moon, Crossed Spears, Rings, Waves.

Commentary

This is quite a busy reading. With so many stones landing face up, there is a lot to unpack and look at. The Star (hopes, dreams, creativity, ambition) and the Moon (obstructions, delays, clouded vision) landed on either side of the Birds, and equal distances away. This formation suggests a balance to be struck or an outcome going one of two ways. The Crossed Spears stone hints at strife, but the absence of the Sickle and the presence of the Rings suggests that strife might be resolved over time. The Waves stone is some way away from the other stones in the reading and sits further back. Being on its own like this suggests a longing for something distant: movement, but subtle and far off. Had it fallen close to the Birds or Waves, the Moon would have suggested sickness of some kind. Given the distance between them, this illness might still come to pass but will be minor if it does.

Conclusion and Actions

Equidistance between the Star and Moon with the Birds stone suggests that the cost of following one's dreams can sometimes mean delays. A dream job is generally harder to land than a job that you are not necessarily passionate about. The key to balancing this equation is the middle stone: the Birds. Here, it speaks of clear communication, messages, and news. This person will avoid roadblocks and delays in their dream job-hunting journey by remaining clear—with themselves and potential employers—about what it is they actually want: the career they are looking for.

The Crossed Spears stone warns of strife, but the danger is softened by the presence of the Rings. Instead, these two stones speak of mending the damage in a relationship and forming strong bonds. This combination encourages the querent to reevaluate relationships with others that might have ended or stagnated. Meanwhile, the Waves stone on its own points to a longing for something as yet far away, though not entirely out of reach. It, along with the Star stone, invites this person to aim high.

Practice, Practice

After connecting with the stones and making your own set in the previous chapters, you should now have a few ideas for performing readings. Experiment, practice, and you will soon find the way that best fits you to get these stones to speak.

Conclusion

As you complete your set of runes, take a moment to sit with the work you've brought to life. Each rune now holds not only the inherent meanings it represents but also a piece of your own journey, infused into every line and mark. In crafting these symbols, you have woven your intentions and energy into each stone, creating the tools that will guide you, reflect you, and grow with you over time. Whether your runes carry the earthy heft of hand-carved lines or the bright glint of inlaid patterns, remember that their power lies not just in their form but in the intention and reverence with which they were created. These runes are now companions, forged by your own hand and spirit, ready to help you explore the many mysteries that lie ahead.

ACKNOWLEDGEMENTS

This work wouldn't be possible without the assistance and encouragement of many. Thank you to all those who aided us in our research and writing, especially Dolores Ashcroft-Nowicki and our editor Heather Greene. Thank you to John Matthews, without whom the foreword would not have been possible. Thank you also to our coven, our upline, and our wonderful community for their unwavering support in everything we do.

Appendix
QUICK REFERENCE GUIDE

Eye: Represents the querant, the signifier. Placed faceup at the start of a reading.

Sun: Strength, growth, positive aspects, energy, fruitfulness.

Moon: Clouded vision, something hidden or not yet come into awareness, dreams, the Otherworld, intuition.

Rings: A bonding or partnership, a link between two situations or people, binding.

Birds: Messages, unexpected news, communication, children, journeys, travel.

Waves: High emotions, fluid situations, movement, the Underworld.

Wheat: Harvest, profit, the reward of hard work (especially physical work), endings, climaxes.

Crossed Spears: Conflict, discord, unrest, clashing energies. Heated parting words. A sign to wait.

Star: Ambition, ideals, energy, inspiration, hope, seeing clearly.

Sickle: Death, monumental change, an abrupt and drastic ending.

BIBLIOGRAPHY

"About Dana Corby." *Patheos* (blog). Accessed October 2024. https://www.patheos.com/blogs/agora/author/dcorby/.

Ashcroft-Nowicki, Dolores. "The Gypsy Runes" In *The Golden Dawn Journal.* Book 1, *Divination.* Edited by Chich Cicero and Sandra Tabatha Cicero. Llewellyn Worldwide, 1994.

Ashcroft-Nowicki, Dolores. "The Gypsy Runes." *Quadriga,* 1977.

Bird, Danny. "Why Did the Soviet Union Adopt the Hammer and Sickle, and How Did It Become a Symbol of Communist Revolution?" *History Extra.* August 7, 2024. https://www.historyextra.com/period/20th-century/hammer-sickle-communism-soviet-symbol-why/.

Blayze. "Gypsy Runes." *Applegrove Online.* Accessed September 2019. http://applegroveonline.com/docs/Curriculum/Module%203%20-%20Lessons%2021%20-%2031/Circle%2030%20Scrying%20And%20Divination%20I/Resources/Gypsy%20Runes.PDF.

Bulfinch, Thomas. *Bulfinch's Mythology.* Avenel Books, 1979.

Chauran, Alexandra. *Runes for Beginners: Simple Divination and Interpretation.* Llewellyn Worldwide, 2016.

"Christian Symbols." Catholic Cemeteries. Accessed October 2024. https://catholic-cemeteries.org/wp-content/uploads/2022/12/Christian-Symbols-FINAL-2022-Wedding-Rings.pdf.

Clinch, A. "Ecstasy and Initiation in the Eleusinian Mysteries." *The Routledge Companion to Ecstatic Experiences in the Ancient World,* edited by Diana Stein, Sarah Kielt Costello, and Karen Polinger Foster. Routledge, 2022.

Corby, Dana. *The Witches' Runes: A Traditional Divination System*. Published by the author, 2018.

Crawford, Jackson, trans. *The Poetic Edda: Stories of the Norse Gods and Heroes*. Hackett Publishing, 2015.

Cromwell, Peter R., Elisabetta Beltrami, and Marta Rampichini. "The Borromean Rings." *The Mathematical Intelligencer* 20, no. 1 (1998): 53–62. https://www.researchgate.net/publication/265313303_The_Borromean_Rings.

Crowther, Patricia. *Lid Off the Cauldron: A Handbook for Witches*. Muller, 1981.

Cunningham, Scott. *Wicca: A Guide for the Solitary Practitioner*. Llewellyn Worldwide, 1989.

Drury, Nevill. *The Dictionary of the Esoteric: More than 3,000 Entries on the Mystical and the Occult Traditions*. Watkins, 2002.

Drury, Nevill. *The Watkins Dictionary of Magic: Over 3,000 Entries on the World of Magical Formulas, Secrets Symbols, and the Occult*. Watkins, 2005.

Editors of Encyclopaedia Britannica. "Dioscuri." Britannica. Updated May 12, 2025. https://www.britannica.com/topic/Dioscuri.

Editors of Encyclopaedia Britannica. "Orion." Britannica. Updated April 12, 2025. https://www.britannica.com/topic/Orion-Greek-mythology.

Editors of Encyclopaedia Britannica. "Osiris." Britannica. Updated March 14, 2025. https://www.britannica.com/topic/Osiris-Egyptian-god.

Evans, Jeff. *Māori Weapons in Pre-European New Zealand*. Reed Books, 2002.

Fitch, Ed. *Magical Rites from the Crystal Well*. Llewellyn Worldwide, 1984.

Fry, Stephen. *Mythos*. The Illustrated Edition. Michael Joseph, 2023.

Fry, Stephen. *Troy: The Greek Myths Reimagined*. Michael Joseph, 2021.

Geddes and Grosset. *Celtic Mythology*. David Dale House, 2002.

Goodman, Simon. "Stones O'Leary." Private documents, 1987.

Green, Marian. *Magic for the Aquarian Age: A Contemporary Textbook of Practical Magical Techniques*. The Aquarian Press, 1983.

Heather, Jennifer. *The Witches' Runes: A Guide to Crafting and Connecting with the Witch Stones*. Heather Publishing, 2024.

"History." Servants of the Light. Accessed February 2025. https://www.servantsofthelight.org/about-sol/history/.

Holmes, Oliver Wendell. *The Autocrat of the Breakfast-Table.* James R. Osgood, 1873.

Homer. *The Iliad: Vintage Classics.* Translated by Caroline Alexander. Penguin Random House. 2015.

Hughes, Kristoffer. *The Book of Celtic Magic: Transformative Teachings from the Cauldron of Awen.* Llewellyn Worldwide, 2014.

Hutton, Ronald. *The Triumph of the Moon: A History of Modern Pagan Witchcraft.* New York: Oxford University Press, 1999.

Hybel, Nils. "The Grain Trade in Northern Europe Before 1350." *The Economic History Review* 55, no. 2 (2002): 219–47. http://www.jstor.org/stable/3091853.

Johnson, Daniel. "Meet Polaris, the North Star." *Sky and Telescope: The Essential Guide to Astronomy.* April 19, 2018. https://skyandtelescope.org/astronomy-news/meet-polaris-the-north-star/.

Knight, Gareth. *A Practical Guide to Qabalistic Symbolism.* Vol. 1, *On the Spheres of the Tree of Life.* Helios Book Service, 1965.

Krauss, Rolf. "The Eye of Horus and the Planet Venus: Astronomical and Mythological References." In *Under One Sky: Astronomy and Mathematics in the Ancient Near East,* edited by John M. Steele and Annette Imhausen. Ugarit-Verlag, 2002.

Lafayllve, Patricia M. *A Practical Heathen's Guide to Asatru.* Llewellyn Worldwide, 2021.

Lienhardt, Godfrey. "Frazer's Anthropology: Science and Sensibility." *Journal of the Anthropological Society of Oxford* 24, no. 1 (1993): 1–12. https://test-anthro.web.ox.ac.uk/sites/default/files/anthro/documents/media/jaso24_1_1993_1_12.pdf.

Lorentzen, Lois Ann. "Santa Muerte: Saint of the Dispossessed, Enemy of Church and State." *Emisférica,* 13, no. 1 (2016). https://hemisphericinstitute.org/en/emisferica-13-1-states-of-devotion.html.

Mackillop, James. *A Dictionary of Celtic Mythology.* Oxford University Press, 1998.

Mastronarde, Donald J. *Preliminary Studies on the Scholia to Euripides.* California Classical Studies, 2017.

Newman, Naomi. "The History of Grain Storage." Milling and Grain. June 8, 2020. https://millingandgrain.com/the-history-of-grain-storage-22328/.

Nock, Judy Ann. *The Modern Witchcraft Guide to Runes: Your Complete Guide to the Divination Power of Runes*. Simon and Schuster, 2022.

Nótári, Tamás. "The Spear as the Symbol of Property and Power in Ancient Rome." *Acta Juridica Hungarica* 48, no. 3 (2007): 231–57. https://doi.org/10.1556/ajur.47.2007.3.2.

"Old-Slavic Symbolism of Bread and Harvest Rituals in Poland." Lamus Dworski. August 6, 2016. https://lamusdworski.wordpress.com/2016/08/06/harvest/.

Opie, Iona, and Moira Tatem, eds. *A Dictionary of Superstitions*. Oxford University Press, 1992.

Ovid. *Metamorphoses: Book VIII*. Penguin Classics, 2014.

Peterson, Joseph H., ed. *The Lesser Key of Solomon: Lemegeton Clavicula Salomonis*. Weiser Books, 2001.

Ragueh, Cherine. "The Blessing of Grain Represented in God 'Nepri' and His Affiliate Gods of Grain: 'Osiris' and 'Renenutet.'" *Journal of Association of Arab Universities for Tourism and Hospitality* 13, no. 2 (2016): 1–22. http://dx.doi.org/10.21608/jaauth.2016.48016.

Rankine, David, and Sorita d'Este. *Practical Qabalah Magick: Working the Magick of the Practical Qabalah and the Tree of Life in the Western Mystery Tradition*. Avalonia, 2009.

Roman, Luke, and Monica Roman. *Encyclopedia of Greek and Roman Mythology*. Infobase Publishing, 2010.

Ryall, Rhiannon. *West Country Wicca: A Journal of the Old Religion*. Phoenix Publishing, 1989.

Sheppard, Susan. *A Witch's Runes: How to Make and Use Your Own Magick Stones*. Citadel Press, 1998.

Signorelli, Fabrizio. "The Power of Grain: Ancient Egypt's Economic and Artistic Legacy." *The Art Insider*, January 9, 2025. https://www.art-insider.com/the-power-of-grain-ancient-egypts-economic-and-artistic-legacy/6845.

Solomon. *The Key of Solomon the King (Clavicula Salomonis)*, translated by Samuel Liddell MacGregor Mathers. Weiser Books, 2016.

Solomon. *The Testament of Solomon.* Translated by Frederick Cornwallis Conybeare. Mockingbird Press, 2017.

"The Stars." Aboriginal Astronomy. 2022. http://www.aboriginalastronomy.com.au/content/topics/stars/.

Sturluson, Snorri. *Edda*, translated by Anthony Faulkes. Everyman, 1987.

"Swords, Crossed." The City of Grove, Oklahoma. Accessed March 2025. https://www.cityofgroveok.gov/building/page/swords-crossed.

Taylor, Tom. "The Devil and the Crossroads: The Legend of Robert Johnson." *Far Out*, January 9, 2021. https://faroutmagazine.co.uk/robert-johnson-myth-devil-crossroads-story/.

Turner, Robert, trans. *Henry Cornelius Agrippa's Fourth Book of Occult Philosophy*. Askin Publishers, 1978. Originally published in 1655.

Valiente, Doreen. *Charge of the Goddess.* Expanded Edition. Centre for Pagan Studies, 2014.

Waite, Arthur Edward. *The Pictorial Key to the Tarot: A Fully Illustrated Guide to What Tarot Is and How to Consult It.* William Rider & Son, 1911.

West, Kate. *The Real Witches' Book of Spells and Rituals.* Element, 2003.

West, Kate. *The Real Witches' Handbook: The Definitive Handbook of Advanced Magical Techniques.* Thorsons, 2001.

"Who Is John Barleycorn? Gruesome Origins and Modern Retellings." *Arcane Alchemy* (blog). September 9, 2020. http://www.arcane-alchemy.com/blog/2020/9/9/who-is-john-barleycorn-gruesome-origins-amp-modern-retellings.

Wilkinson, Richard H. *Reading Egyptian Art: A Hieroglyphic Guide to Ancient Egyptian Painting and Sculpture.* Thames and Hudson, 1992.

Williams, Victoria. *Celebrating Life Customs Around the World: From Baby Showers to Funerals.* ABC-CLIO, 2016.

Winter, Josephine. *Witchcraft Discovered: Magic, Ritual, and Enchantment for the Head, Hands, and Heart.* Llewellyn Worldwide, 2023.